SHOW HORSES AN

WHAT MAKES A

SHOW HORSES AND PONIES: WHAT MAKES A WINNER

Phyllis Hinton
and
John Nestle

DAVID & CHARLES : NEWTON ABBOT

0 7153 6277 1

© Phyllis Hinton and John Nestle 1973
© Photographs John Nestle

Set in 11/13point Plantin
and printed in Great Britain
by W J Holman Limited Dawlish
for David & Charles (Holdings) Limited
South Devon House Newton Abbot Devon

Foreword

From His Grace, the Duke of Beaufort

I have known John Nestle for a number of years, and
I have always considered his writings and especially
his photographs to be first rate in every way. I look
forward with confidence to *Show Horses and Ponies:
What Makes a Winner*, which I am sure will prove
of great interest.

MASTER

To Walter Case,
Editor of *Horse and Hound*

Contents

Illustrations

9

ILLUSTRATIONS

(*All photographs in this book are copyright to John Nestle*)

I

The Art of Showing

What *does* make a horse or pony win in the show ring? This question has been asked by many people and is so complex that it is not easy to answer quickly. In fact you will receive a stimulating variety of replies if you put it to several different judges—apt, amusing, helpful or derisive. Added together they will give you an idea of the points needed in the winning animal and also of the many aspects of judging. Judging is no easy task.

The object of the model show classes, as opposed to the performance competitions, is to discover the horse which is the best of his type, whether that type is classified as a hunter, a hack, a pony, or indeed an exhibit in any specified event. He should be true to type—even the horse with the best conformation, manners and movement may not be as suitable for a particular class as the one which does not measure up to him in other respects.

This presents problems, but unless the horse is too obviously unsuitable to the class in which he is entered he, as the best

11

animal there, must win; if there is little to choose between them then the result is anybody's guess. It may depend on the judge's particular liking; and also on a number of factors which the onlooker probably cannot assess from the ringside which may include manners and way of going.

The qualities which make a horse or pony what he is are largely brought about by his breeding, sometimes as the result of the knowledge, experience and flair of his breeder, sometimes partly by chance. Added to this one cannot ignore the effect of his surroundings and the way in which he has been looked after during the early months and years of his life.

If your horse is true to type those qualities needed for his particular work must predominate. For example, if he is a hunter he must have strength, courage and good action—in other words, his limbs, joints, feet, shoulders, and particularly his back must be such as will enable him to carry out his specific job.

This principle applies in every single section or class into which horses and ponies are divided and, in addition, a certain brilliance and beauty is expected in the model show horse, as well as manners, training and personality, which are not quite so essential in his more ordinary but possibly very capable brother. A practical appreciation or realisation of these very simple facts will help exhibitors who have not had much experience of showing or ringcraft. It will also help everyone who enjoys watching the various classes to understand more easily what it is all about—how and why the animals are judged.

We hope that the photographs we have chosen to illustrate these chapters will not only please all those who love horses but will add to their knowledge and understanding of an animal who has been so closely associated with our own progress throughout the centuries. They will also emphasise and explain the various points which he should possess if he is to win in the show ring.

One cannot overlook the human element in the production of the show horse. First of all there is the breeder, who may or may not exhibit him in the in-hand classes as a youngster, or even still own him if and when he competes under saddle. Many breeders sell their young stock as yearlings or two-year-olds but at least they have introduced them to humanity and, we hope, to proper handling.

These youngsters are usually schooled and produced in the ridden by the same person, at others they have a different ately few people show a horse or pony under saddle on more than a very few occasions when they are still only three, as mentally and physically they are not ready for this kind of life and can very easily be spoilt. An occasional short outing does no harm, provided they have a lightweight on their backs, as it gets them used to the excitement of the show ground in preparation for the real business the following season.

This brings us to their contact with those people who actually train and produce them, and to those who ride them in the ring. Sometimes they are both trained, produced and ridden by the same person, at others they have a different rider. These human contacts may be professionals or amateurs and many of them are exceptionally gifted all-round horsemen or women, while others are very successful with only one type of animal.

Why is it that a horse or pony will go more easily for one person than he will for another who may appear to be equally gifted? An interesting question, hard to answer. Is it an instinctive response, similar to our own human reactions to one another? What can be astonishing is the result of changing over two riders, each on quite good horses. If one of them is well up in theory but lacking in imagination or understanding he will probably run into difficulties whereas the natural horseman will have no trouble.

13

But whether you are planning to show a horse or pony yourself, or just enjoy watching other people do it, remember the hard work that they and their assistants have had to put in either breeding or else finding and buying the right animal; correctly feeding, caring for and training it; bringing it to the show, which may have meant getting up at about 3 am; producing it in all its glory on the show ground, possibly exercising and settling it down in these alien surroundings; and finally showing it at its best when actually in the ring, ensuring that it moves freely and tranquilly as it enters, that it is sufficiently gay but completely obedient, that it 'uses' itself to the full and strides out well and that whoever is riding or leading it never fails to catch the judges' or stewards' commands.

Showing is an art—that is what makes it so interesting—and the good showman must be a great artist with a sense of the theatre. Perhaps one of the most important secrets of success in the show ring is to be a good horseman and to be objective. In short to know what has to be done and to do it with good heart, realistically and instinctively but impersonally. After all, you are exhibiting your horse, not yourself, and if this is done properly you will have no time to worry, because the good horseman is concentrating on his horse and his surroundings, on what he knows he has to do, and how to cope with any expected or unexpected reactions so that he will lose any nervous fussiness and end by enjoying himself. This is an excellent thing as a horse quickly senses anxiety, fear and doubt.

There have been some great artists in the show ring, many with so much knowledge and understanding of a horse's mentality that their very practical 'secrets of the trade' have helped them to deal successfully with the thousand and one problems which can arise.

Hard work, beauty, enjoyment, thrills, great generosity—and great meanness, too—as well as a very real sense of good

14

sportsmanship, are all characteristics of the show world; but extreme jealousy, ruthlessness, bitterness, malice and unfair criticism also exist. In fact, the strange and colourful world of the show ring has much in common with that of the theatre.

Perhaps one of the most notable of our professional show-ring riders today is David Tatlow, son of Harold Tatlow—'Tat', himself a lifelong showman and producer of so many famous hacks. On one occasion at the British Timken show, held at Duston, Northampton, 'Tat', his two sons, David and Roy, and his daughter-in-law Barbara, all rode in one class. This must certainly be a record.

As well as showing horses in the summer David is a successful National Hunt trainer. At the end of his second season he had nineteen races and £8,403 to his credit. He rode 127 winners in point-to-points and was champion for four consecutive years. His father never forced showing on him as a child, but he loved his days as a member of the North Warwickshire Branch of the Pony Club, and still gives a lot of time to instructing at the various rallies.

He learnt a lot from the various horses who came to his father's yard for breaking and schooling. The immensely individual character of each horse makes it a nonsense to hold too rigid a belief in any one theory of equitation. A strong seat in the saddle, light hands and an ability to understand and adapt to the horse one rides is the secret of successful horsemanship. David really loves horses and is unremitting in his care of them—they are his life. And he is one of the few people who will show a hack or hunter equally well. Annie Davy, who used to work with Count Robert Orssich, was another.

Talking of David Tatlow and his family—it is unusual that so large a proportion of them should be gifted with horses—reminds one of the great debt one owes the showmen of today and of the last fifty years. They were all perfectionists in their own way, for example Dick Pritchard, Harry Bonner, Sam

15

Marsh and Robert Orssich to name but a few. They helped to create a high standard in the choosing, training and presentation of the show horse and laid a firm foundation on which we can build.

Now the modern way of life calls for certain adjustments if horse shows are to continue but this does not affect the first principles. We need, perhaps to model some of our classes on those in use in Canada and the United States, especially the working hunter and working pony, which are so practical and so popular over there. They can be a better economic proposition to many riders in Britain today than some of the model show classes and are of greater interest to the average onlooker once he understands the points on which they are judged.

The successful showman or woman is indeed a dedicated person and another example of how the love of horses runs in families is supplied by the Bullens. Take for instance the eldest daughter, Jennie Bullen, now Mrs A. G. Loriston-Clarke, who throughout her life has shown herself well able to school and exhibit successfully the dressage horse, the hack and the child's pony or indeed to take part in almost any kind of class you like to suggest. In addition to these time-consuming activities she thoroughly enjoys riding in the New Forest countryside with her family, as well as hunting and also schooling her racehorse stallion, Xenocles, who is by Nearula out of a Dante mare. She rode Kadett for Mrs Steele in the Grand Prix dressage of the 1972 Olympic Games at Munich, putting up a highly creditable performance.

Jennie's mother, the late Anne Bullen, a gifted equestrian artist, had a great talent for fostering the children's natural love of horses and giving them the correct training in competitive riding. There were six of them and Michael, Jennie, Jane and Sarah are the four who are the best-known in connection with showing and horse trials. They enjoyed it all tremendously, growing very strong and physically tough;

16

unassuming, sound young riders with a sporting instinct, neither self-willed nor self-seeking but thoroughly interested in what they did and in good horsemastership, or, shall we say, the care of their animals.

Jane Bullen won the Badminton Horse Trials with Our Nobby in 1968, while she was training very wholeheartedly as a hospital nurse. She was chosen to compete as a member of the British 1968 Olympic Three-Day-Event team, and she and Our Nobby were wonderful partners. Incidentally Our Nobby was retired from competitive events after this very considerable effort and lives a more peaceful but happy life. Horses are real people to the Bullens, with idiosyncrasies which must be understood and respected.

Michael Bullen took a very effective part in Pony Club events throughout his boyhood, later riding most competently various horses belonging to Col and Mrs V. D. S. Williams at Badminton on numerous occasions. Now he is an important member of the firm J. A. Peden Ltd, and successfully arranges the transport of horses of every description all over the world. Sarah Bullen rode and showed a considerable number of both ponies and horses.

Their father, the late Col J. F. S. Bullen, was himself a great horseman, trained at Weedon. He won thirty-eight consecutive point-to-points on his horse, Gold Dust, in the West Country, mostly over banks. Col Bullen had a wonderful way with horses and would ride many of the difficult horses and ponies at their home at Catherston and within a few days even the most awkward would go kindly. He was very much a guiding light and a consistent help to his entire family in their riding, whether for fun, in competitions or during displays such as the Cattistock Musical Ride, the Jorrocks and Aylesbury Steeplechase at the Horse of the Year Shows, and many others.

Both he and his wife had a great eye for a horse or pony

17

and the gift of spotting them in the rough. Royal Show, Criban Bumble, Coed Coch Pryderi (later to go to America), Coed Coch Penpali, Silver Moon and the exceptionally beautiful Palomino stallion, Bubbly, all took part in these displays—it is no wonder that they were such good-mannered happy ponies, ideal for children.

What was the particular secret of the success of these two present-day stars of the show ring, David Tatlow and Jennie Loriston-Clarke, and indeed, of other great showmen of the recent past? Their remarkable understanding of horses who, to them, are not creatures of another world, is part of the reason for their success. Add to this their unremitting work in connection with horses from their childhood upwards which through sheer contact with the animal has taught them so much, and which from force of habit has become instinctive and not so difficult or exhausting as it would be to the less experienced and less fit individual.

Another thing they have in common is that their family is horse-minded and they have therefore taken horses and ponies for granted from their earliest childhood. They are able to appreciate that no matter how long they live they will always find something more to learn and this exhilarates them. Their gift for horsemanship resembles that of any other artist whose particular talent is not something which can ever be acquired —it is born in them—although it may mean immensely hard work to bring it to perfection; it opens up endless possibilities which otherwise they might never have visualised.

Finally, and this is one of the most important things of all, they know exactly what is wanted in each class, and they try to produce just that. Not only have they studied the schedules and the rules of the event, but they know it by observation and experience. They know what the judges are looking for, as we shall try to explain in the ensuing pages, and also just why they ask for various movements. They take very good care, every minute of the time, to produce their animal to the best advantage, often making the horse look as if they did it all with the minimum of effort on their part. They never miss a point, or even half a point, but make no fuss about it because they are literally and instinctively 'with it' all the time, and are always ready to cope or adjust. And they know all the 'tricks of the trade', the small things which can produce the best results with the least difficulty.

In addition to Jennie and David there are, of course, other very gifted professional and amateur riders today, both in and out of the model show ring—show-jumping and horse trials do not come into this particular category. But we hope that what we have said about these two very well-known and completely modern exponents of good horsemanship will interest and assist everyone who wants to know something of the art of showmanship.

There are also many people with less time or opportunity who can get a great deal of fun and a certain amount of success out of competing in the show ring even if they never hit the high spots. They are important because they help to keep the wheels turning and without them the classes would lose half their interest. Not only is there much to be learnt by riding in the company of the expert but it can also be good fun and there is always the chance that you and your horse may find yourself at the right end of the line—an experience one would not like to miss. The excitement alone is worth the prize money!

The scene is changing to a certain extent and new and different classes are attracting our attention, but it is to be hoped that we shall continue to breed the best type of horse; to maintain our good pasture land where the young stock can mature and never fail to take the infinite trouble, patience and hard work which go to the production both of the good horse and the good horsemaster or stable manager.

It is an interesting thought that the really good judges can often make clear to spectators what they are looking for by the way they set about their judging. The late Mr Horace Smith when discussing this vital subject used to say that a judge should always try to have some kind of uniformity in his placings, judge to a pattern, so that the first half dozen horses are of much the same stamp.

A final tip from John Nestle. He says 'Were I asked to give one short sentence of advice to anyone just going into the ring to judge I should say, "Look at each animal with the eye of an artist. You will soon see if his proportions, his symmetry are as they should be and if this is so you will usually find that he is a good horse." '

The late Lady Wentworth wrote in *The Authentic Arabian Horse* (1962) that 'beauty, symmetry and balance are evidence of efficiency'.

2

Points to Remember When Showing Your Horse

In this chapter we hope to help and interest those who lack experience in the actual process of exhibiting their horse or pony and also the ringside observer who is not quite sure what it is all about.

Our first piece of advice is this; watch all classes, not just the event to which you are particularly attracted, and learn from each one. At first you may be a little confused as you will see so many age groups and types of animal at various and differing shows but gradually a pattern will emerge. Pay attention if you can to the stallions and brood mares and the type of progeny they produce, to the classes for young stock and, later to the finished article, the show hack or hunter or pony. You will soon learn to recognise the good and bad points and the essential differences.

Watch the real exponents of the art of showing. It is not difficult to spot the expert, whether in a ridden or an in-hand event. He will have a certain air of efficiency and yet he will make everything appear unexpectedly easy. Then find out who these people are, and do not be afraid to speak to them, choosing the right time, when they are not in the ring. If by ill chance you strike the wrong moment do not lose heart, just find out when it will be convenient for you to have a word with them; but never attempt to do so as they are preparing for, or are about to take part in a class. Usually the top exhibitors are very friendly providing they are not busy and will be glad to give a sound answer to an intelligent question, or explain a point which is not clear to you.

We are of the opinion that showing is very much like going in for an examination. You must have the right answers and you must present your animal which is to be examined very efficiently. For instance, it is of primary importance that you and your horse should be in good trim and well turned-out. The combination of horse and rider will then be agreeable to the eye. Never forget that you are out to please the judge and that every detail of the quality and appearance of your exhibit counts. Naturally the nicer the clothes of the exhibitor and the tack of the horse the better, but all we are asking for now is that they should be neat, clean and correct. And this applies equally to the in-hand classes, no matter whether it involves a brood mare, a yearling in a show head collar or a foal in a natty little foal slip. Those who lead them should also be neatly if simply dressed.

In a ridden class, particularly at the big shows, it is as well to use a properly designed show saddle, which is cut fairly straight to display your animal's overall conformation, particularly the shoulder, to advantage. These are expensive to buy and obviously must fit your horse to perfection, but sometimes they can be obtained second-hand, possibly from an

22

exhibitor who is giving up showing.

Throughout your 'examination' you must use your wits and good manners to make the examining judge's task as easy as possible. For instance, when the horses are lined up for his inspection take care that they are standing straight and are not too close together, otherwise it will be awkward for him to pass between them, and certainly impossible to get a clear view of each. So tactfully ask the owner of the animal standing next to yours to move over, to give a little leeway as it may not have occurred to him that this was necessary.

Be at attention all the time, having shortened or lengthened the stirrups in readiness for the judge to ride your horse if it is standing near the top of a ridden event. And afterwards remove the saddle in preparation for the run-down in hand. Possibly an assistant will bring a linen rubber to give your horse a quick polish before he is led out in front of the judge. And make him stand on a straight line, alert and using all four legs, not trailing or resting one.

We have suggested that if any query arises in your mind when you are watching a top class exhibitor you should ask this individual to explain it to you. In the same way the majority of judges will reply gladly to any question you may wish to put to them after an event has been judged. But do ask your questions politely, not critically or bitterly, if you want a reply which is worth having. We personally have always been delighted to explain anything which puzzled an exhibitor or onlooker when we had finished judging, providing we were convinced that there was no malice behind the question. Judging can be a very rewarding and also a very thankless task.

It may happen that you show your horse or pony several times before the same judge, but never with any success, and you wonder what is wrong. It is possible that the judge will be able to tell you although the answer may not be a very palatable one. Equally he may give you a tip which will be of real use to you in the future. Whatever he says, do be wise enough to accept it in good faith.

A judge's decision is bound to revolve to a certain extent round his own personal leaning towards a certain stamp of animal, its way of going, or other relevant factors. If yours does not quite come into this category why not show him under another judge and see what happens? This piece of advice may give some rise to argument as the principles of how to judge a good horse should not be too elastic, but you must remember that type does come into judging, that we all have certain innate preferences for some point in conformation, movement or type and when competition is close this will almost certainly affect the final issue.

It is always possible that subconsciously a judge may favour a horse which he has known, owned or bred. This can also work in reverse. Instinctively he may be too critical of such an animal, knowing very well that he is likely to be accused of favouritism, of accepting bribery, or of having sold the horse or pony on the implied (not stated) assumption that obviously it will win if he is judging.

Therefore, to protect both judge and public various societies have issued their own rules. The Hunters Improvement and National Light Horse Breeding Society states:

The onus of a horse being exhibited in a class by a person who has had a financial interest in the animal, or which has stood in his own stable etc, must be on the exhibitor. The exhibitor will know who is judging from the schedule, whereas the judge will not know which animals are coming before him until he arrives in the ring. If there is an unforeseen change of judge then he should stand down from the class.

The practice of a judge exhibiting horses for someone and then, at a later date, judging these horses for the same owner, is very much deprecated by the Society. All judges are subject to re-election to the Panel annually.

The British Show Pony Society points out to its members in rule 13 that 'No person may deliberately enter and show a pony under a judge who is known to have bred, sold, or produced that pony. Panel judges are asked to take particular note of Rule 13.'

Learn the right way to show your horse and do it yourself instead of asking the expert to do it for you. You will then find that the other competitors are more friendly. Up to a point this applies to all classes but especially to the in-hand events, which are not difficult to handle, providing you have plenty of common sense. But in contradiction to this, if you are exhibiting a valuable young animal at the beginning of the season for the first time, then let some more gifted showman or woman do this for you. When the horse has settled to the job and, above all, made his reputation, you can take him over if you wish to do so. Unless you are experienced as well as having a talent for showing, it is unlikely that you will achieve very much with an unknown horse when he makes his debut . . . particularly in strong competition.

The spirit of competition is very strong today, because of the costs and trouble involved, the fact that a rosette may add to the value of the animal and because some exhibitors have an almost pathological will to win. For this reason and also because there are hooligans about even on a show ground, never leave a horse or pony which is a consistent winner, or who is likely to be picked for championship honours, unattended. No matter whether he is stabled, boxed or picketed. There have been one or two nasty instances when a show horse has been blemished in some way or even seriously injured. It is also as well not to keep him on the show ground longer than is necessary, but to take him back to the comfort and safety of his own home as soon as possible. And do not forget that there are plenty of pilferers around who will pinch anything from a raincoat to a saddle.

At the bigger shows the preliminary judging is often done in another ring before the horses file into the main ring for the final decision to be made. If a class is particularly well-filled those which will not be placed in the front line are sometimes invited to leave the scene of action, instead of hanging about to no purpose. But unless instructed to do so a competitor should not withdraw from the event without first asking the judge's permission and explaining the reason for the request—it maybe that he or she wishes to get ready for another class.

If you decide to take part either in a ridden or an in-hand event at a medium-sized show, the following programme will be of use.

First make a list (and keep this permanently handy) of what you yourself will want with you, and also what the horse will require. This will help considerably in checking the equipment before you move off. Leave out nothing, no matter how small, and include each separate item of the grooming kit, scissors, spare bandages, cotton wool, needle and thread, dust sheet, bucket for water, and so on. As this book does not attempt to cover stable management and the actual feeding of each type of horse we shall not include times and quantities of feeds, watering etc, but be careful never to overlook these vital points, especially after your horse has finished his work in the ring.

One assumes that whether ridden or shown in-hand he will have been consistently and thoroughly groomed, that his feet and shoes are in good order, and that final attention to every detail is given on the day of the show. Full instructions as to mane plaiting, water marks (diamonds), tail trimming and so on are given in Chapter 5. In special cases the manes are plaited, not too tightly, on the evening before the show, but they will look much neater if done shortly before the horse goes in the ring. If travelling by box use a tail bandage to protect the tail from rubbing. Bandages and knee pads are advisable, the former preventing strain on the legs, and the latter the knees from damage.

Be sure to allow more than ample time to arrive at the show; so many things can occur which could delay you. If you have travelled by box this will give you a chance to limber up and exercise your horse, to get him accustomed to his new surroundings, as well as finally polished and saddled up in preparation for his class. It will also help you to settle down, relax, dress yourself, go to the secretary's tent to announce your arrival, possibly collect your number and in any case confirm your class and find out whether the show is running on time. Report to your collecting ring steward, check the time of the class (this can be important) and make sure that you are available to enter the collecting ring directly the class is called.

Be careful not to get too close to other horses in the collecting ring—accidents can and do happen—and keep your horse moving quietly round, do not let him get bored. The same principle applies when you enter the judging ring so keep your distance within reason. Remember that the judge must be able to see your exhibit, whether ridden or in-hand, so do not behave as if it were a pair class and remain alongside another animal—keep back or else pass him—otherwise it is impossible for the judge to get a good view of either of you. Listen carefully to the steward's commands, or if there is a ring guard in action pay attention to the sound of his horn, exhorting you to increase or decrease speed, to change your pace. Whether trotting, cantering or galloping be sure to use all the ring; do not cut the corners.

The judge often asks the steward to call the horses in roughly in the order in which he thinks they may eventually be placed, but this does not mean that the placings will not be changed when he has had a chance to ride them, or to inspect them at close quarters. Occasionally the entire class is called in just as it is and no attempt is made to place the animals until later on: and in a big class it is sometimes easier to call in the less good animals first, to enable the judge to observe more carefully those which he thinks might be chosen for the front line. Whatever the case, when your turn comes take care that there is sufficient room between you and the horses on either side. Relax to a certain extent, but remain alert. Smile your sweetest at the judge but do not engage in conversation, except in response to any questions he may ask you.

You may be invited to give an individual show. Why? Because he wishes to see if your horse is obedient, responsive to the aids and has achieved a fair but not necessarily advanced standard in training. He may ask you to give a short display of your own devising, or he may suggest that you walk, trot, canter, circle and possibly rein back. Never in an individual show attempt more than your horse can carry out efficiently —and this includes you yourself—or inevitably the movement will be performed incorrectly or sloppily, thereby drawing attention to the sad fact that the horse is not as well schooled as you would like the judge to believe. A short display, given at no great distance away from the judge and properly carried out, will earn more good marks than a long boring one ill-performed. When you return to your place remember not to pass too close to any of the other horses' heels or you will annoy them, probably get kicked for your carelessness and cause havoc among those standing fairly close to you.

Further advice on individual shows will be given in the various chapters referring to hacks, ponies and so on.

It is quite possible that the judge may wish to ride, to try out your horse. In the United States and Canada there are few model show classes in which the judges ride the horses. In the United Kingdom and Ireland however they want to test for themselves the horse's obedience, his willingness to go well for a different rider, his degree of training and whether he is a good, that is to say a comfortable, ride. They can assess his capabilities, possibly his temperament, more easily from his back than on the ground and they may like to try him out in their own way to discover his reactions, to prove that he is an honest, straightforward ride.

It will save time and be of real assistance to the judge if you shorten or lengthen the stirrup leathers to the approximate length likely to be required, make sure that your horse stands still until instructed to move off and hold the stirrup leather on the far side while the judge is actually in the process of mounting, unless of course you have thrown him up. Watch what the judge does as he rides, notice your horse's reactions and learn all you can. One thing is sure: that horses will always go better for some people than others, for an experienced, educated horseman with good hands may be a far better judge of horseflesh than a highly polished performer whose terms of reference are possibly limited and who has little experience or flair for judging.

Judging is no easy job, and requires a certain technique and pattern, as well as the seeing eye, tact, strength of character and an ability to adapt to the circumstances of the day and place.

The following interesting and rather unusual story refers to an occasion when one of us—John Nestle in fact—was judging the hack classes at the Cape Show in South Africa. 'In one of the events I chose a thoroughbred horse which obviously must have started its career as a racehorse. I was very favourably impressed by the individual display it had given in the hands of its owner-rider. When I rode the horse myself I noticed that it had a rather tender mouth but was otherwise truly responsive to the aids. Eventually I awarded the hack championship to this animal and, incidentally, I was well pleased when told at a later date that it became champion again the following year at the same show under a Rhodesian judge.'

'When I had finished judging these events the owner who, naturally, was pleased that her horse had gone so well for me, asked if I would like to visit it in its box on the show ground. This I did, and she drew my attention to the fact that this animal had had a serious accident to its mouth on a train journey—the jaw had been broken and plated and two teeth stopped. Had I been heavy-handed or ridden it without a certain sympathy it would have given me an impossible ride and might even have tried to deposit me on the ground. This is an example of how an experienced horseman could possibly have the edge over a more impressive rider with less actual experience. It is true that some people might argue that because of this animal's particularly sensitive mouth it should never have been made champion, by myself or anyone else, but it went very well for me and for its owner, and as a horse it was certainly the best animal present on the day.'

To return to the programme of proceedings in the ring. If, when you have reached this stage the judge is still interested in your horse you will be instructed to remove the saddle, or have it removed by your assistant who will now join you, and this is the moment to give your horse a polish with a stable rubber. Incidentally, some people say that when you are turning out a horse to look his best in the ring a final rub with a piece of silk brings up the brightest sheen! The steward will then ask you to lead your horse out in front of the judge and stand him on a parallel line so that he can obtain a good broadside view. This will also enable the spectators to have a good look at him.

You may wonder why the judge wants to see him without

the saddle. In a marginal case this often helps one make a decision because a horse can look very different with nothing on his back—a good horse will look even better without his saddle but the weaknesses of an indifferent one will be more apparent. Perhaps his neck is set on badly, his withers are even less good than you thought, his body a shade shallow, his quarters a little weak, his loins the same and his back rather long. A clever showman usually knows his horse's weaknesses and will endeavour to cover them up, to mitigate them. For instance, if the horse's back is a shade on the long side he will have his saddle placed slightly to the rear and will also incline his own body back slightly or wear a rather long coat when showing the horse off. These tactics do not deceive the really experienced judge.

While the horse is standing without his saddle the judge may have a final look for any possible defects of body, limbs or feet and may perhaps glance at his teeth if he feels it necessary to check his age. The horse may have slightly curby or otherwise weak hocks—not very noticeable and not an unsoundness but something which can give rise to trouble. He may be slightly tied in *below* the knee. This should never be confused with 'over at the knee', which is not a fault. He may be either a little too narrow or too wide in the chest, or his elbows may be tucked in too close to his body, which will make it difficult for him to use his shoulder to the best advantage. He may show signs of scars, perhaps caused by brushing, to combat which, his shoes may have been feather-edged. If a horse brushes, his joints are bound to suffer.

It is unlikely that any of these faults are particularly bad or the horse would not be shown at all, but they are points which, together with many others, have to be weighed up and which may not be easy to spot from the ringside.

Leave your horse's head free as much as possible—you should have taught him to stand—but first make sure that he is poised on all four legs, showing himself off to advantage and is alert and interested. Perhaps you will have some tit-bit you can give him or, as a last resort, a handful of grass.

When you are asked to run him down, which will enable the judge to watch his action, try and walk away on a straight line and do not go too far. Then turn him neatly, always with his quarters inwards and under control, ie with yourself on the outside of the circle. Do not just swing to right or left and pull him after you, turn *him* and follow his shoulder round, thus making quite a small circle. Go immediately into a trot and run beside him, if possible on a level with his shoulder but not too close. Practise this before you have to do it in the show ring. Trot slowly but steadily on a straight line past the judge, who may want to have a look at his action from the rear.

What is the judge looking for? Whatever it is, do not obstruct his view by getting your own body in his line of vision, or by holding the reins too close to the horse's chin. This is what a crafty dealer would do if he were trying to sell a horse which was not a good mover or not quite sound. In other words, trot him with as free a rein as you reasonably can and try to keep on a parallel line with his shoulder. The judge may want to see if he moves freely, well, and absolutely straight, does not go too close or too wide in front or behind; does not show his feet out sideways, thus 'dishing'; does not place one foot slightly crosswise in front of the other ie 'plaiting'; or, in fact, whether his action is good or bad and if he has any special weaknesses.

Having carried out any instructions given you by the steward and taken care to make it as easy as possible for both the judge and the spectators, who after all have paid for this privilege, to have a good look at your horse, then return quietly to your place and saddle up as soon as you can. You may be asked to move into a better position in the line-up or you may be demoted; or requested to ride with other runners-up in a

Page 33 (*above*) Dargee after winning the supreme championship at the Arab Horse Show at 15 years of age; (*below*) Darjeel (sire Dargee, dam Rajjela), stallion champion and male champion at the same show at a later date. Note the small, noble head with the dished face; the strong graceful neck; the good withers; the short, strong back; the length from hip to buttock and good workmanlike limbs that can also be seen in his handsome son Darjeel

Page 34 (*above*) Majal (sire Indian Magic, dam Mifaria), at 3 years old. Bred by Lady Anne Lytton, he was reserve junior male champion at the Arab Show. He too has a body of great strength and invaluable potential with limbs which will stand up to hard work. Note his strong back and hocks; (*below*) the graceful chestnut mare Nerinora (sire Oran, dam Nerina), originally owned by the Crabbet Arabian Stud. Note the beautiful proportions of her body and limbs. She is full of quality but nowhere does she display weakness or heaviness

small circle round the judge before you are called into your final position and the rosettes are awarded.

One of the first requisites in any type of prize-winning horse or pony is an air of quality, which is usually the result of breeding from good stock. Never imagine that a flashy horse, or a 'flat-catcher', whose outward appearance or 'presence' attracts the eye is an example of quality. Either of these animals may have any number of weak points and a chancy temperament for good measure. The same can apply to some highly bred or inbred animals. Remember that the 'blood-weed' of gallant appearance but little substance is a worthless creature.

Quality gives any horse or pony a certain something, an air of power because of the perfection of his proportions, his good bone structure, lack of all coarseness and consequent grace. These attributes will put him just ahead of another animal who may have many good points but not much refinement. He has within himself the ingredients of the great champion. But do not be put off if your own horse does not quite reach these heights, has that little bit less quality—as long as he has plenty of sense and soundness he will probably do very well for you. Classic top class champions are few and far between.

Sometimes it happens that the judge is undecided, or if there are two judges that they are not in complete agreement over the merits of, let us say, the first and second horse. If this is so they may decide to have the two in question stood in line, one behind the other without their saddles, and compare points, but such procedure is infrequent. In the case of a disagreement between the judges it is usual to send for a referee to decide on the placing of the two horses in question, without reference to the position of any other horse in the same class. The referee should not be informed which judge favours which horse.

One of the most depressing jobs any judge has to face is

C

when he feels compelled to put an old champion down to an oncoming young horse, particularly if the old horse has been at the top for many years and seems automatically to regard it as his rightful place—as his owner certainly will! He may still be a wonderful looker and a good mover but obviously his day is ended and he must soon begin or already has, in fact, begun to go downhill. From the point of view of value alone he is not as good a horse as he was in previous years or as the younger animal who takes his place at the head of the line.

Is the judge right to put him down? If the younger animal is equally good, the answer must perforce be yes. This is only fair to other exhibitors who may have waited their turn for a long while and deserve to get a look in and it encourages the breeding of new, good stock. But it is a hard and difficult thing to do. We all hate to see any old friend relegated to a lesser place and know that his day is done. But supposing the younger horse is not quite up to the standard of the older one, then the veteran should retain his glory. There is, however, much divergence of opinion on this point. The answer depends on just how much difference there is between them, as well as the kind of class in which they are being shown. Many exhibitors wisely retire their champions while they are still at their peak.

Good judging helps to set the standard and encourages the breeding of the right type of animal and because of this a judge of wide experience whose background is horses is someone to be greatly valued. Specialised knowledge is not enough in itself. Years ago a horseman of considerable standing deplored the fact that stable management will become a lost art if we are not careful and one must agree with him. The constant need for speed is its worst enemy.

Occasionally you will spot a lame horse in the ring, or one which is not absolutely sound. This is not always easy to deal with particularly if the apparent unsoundness is very slight.

Sometimes horses have a rather misleading action; or a slightly awkward way of going; or are 'bridle lame', not happy in the mouth and not on the bit; or again a horse may move straight for a few paces, then drop his head for a few. In any case this is a matter for the veterinary surgeon to decide.

The ruling given by the British Show Pony Society has been found as practical as any. It says: 'If in the opinion of the judge, a pony is considered to be unsound, the exhibitor should be given the option of withdrawing the exhibit from the class or asking that the official veterinary surgeon should examine the pony. The veterinary surgeon's decision is final.'

In Canada they have a very simple way of dealing with the possibility of lameness. If a judge is of the opinion that one of the horses or ponies in his class is not absolutely sound he asks for a veterinary surgeon to stand beside him, watch them all on the move and himself pick out the defaulting animal. This method is not described in the rule book but it is stated 'The examination of a horse in the ring shall be done as inconspicuously as possible and in such a manner as not to draw public attention thereto. The co-operation of judges to this end is required.' Having indicated that each recognised show must have a qualified veterinarian present, it adds that 'If a veterinarian is not immediately available the judge's decision is final in respect to a horse in competition.'

To finish this chapter let us consider the heights of the horses in the various classes covered by the Joint Measurement Scheme.

Show hunters have no height limit except in the case of small hunters, which must not exceed 15 hands 2 inches high. A hand is four inches. Working hunters are often classified in a show schedule as 15.2hh and over.

Hack classes are for those exceeding 14.2hh but not exceeding 15hh, and exceeding 15hh but not exceeding 15.3hh. Ladies' hacks, to be ridden side-saddle, must exceed 14.2hh but not exceed 15.3hh.

The show classification of a cob usually states that it must exceed 14.2hh but not exceed 15.3hh.

For children's ponies the main height limits are those not exceeding 12.2hh, exceeding 12.2hh but not exceeding 13.2hh, exceeding 13.2hh but not exceeding 14.2hh. Further details with reference to pony classes are given in Chapter 8. Mountain and moorland ponies are usually registered with their respective breed societies, which determine their height limits.

It is advisable to hold a certificate issued by the Joint Measurement Scheme (see p189), otherwise your horse or pony may have to be measured on the show ground. Most shows accept these certificates, although there are a few exceptions.

Life certificates are issued for horses or ponies of six years old or over. These may only be measured between 1 April and 30 September, except when an objection may overlap this period. The right is reserved to have an animal re-measured at any time that may be deemed necessary by two referees appointed by the Royal College of Veterinary Surgeons.

Annual certificates are issued for ponies of four and five years. No certificates are issued to animals under four years old. Again, the right to re-measure an animal is reserved.

Every horse and pony must be named and any change of name must be notified by the owner.

In the event of a sale or transfer of an animal holding a measurement certificate, the certificate will become null and void after seven days unless it is sent in for amendment and is re-issued by the secretary. In the event of the death of an animal holding a certificate this must be sent to the secretary for destruction.

An official list of approved veterinary surgeons, who have

consented to act as official measurers, has been adopted. All have received the necessary forms and instructions, and owners requiring animals measured should communicate direct with any of the official measurers.

The measurement fee is payable by the owner direct to the official measurer. The registration fee is payable to the secretary of the Joint Measurement Scheme and is 50p for an annual certificate or £1 for a certificate for an animal over six years.

On receipt of the measurement form from the measurer and the fee of £1, or 50p for an annual certificate per animal from the owner, an official measurement certificate will be issued by the secretary, Joint Measurement Scheme.

The following measurement rules have been adopted:

1 The veterinary surgeon issuing the certificate has the responsibility of ensuring that the stick he uses is an accurate one; it must be fitted with a spirit level and be shod with metal.

2 All four legs to be perpendicular to the ground, the forelegs in line.

3 The poll shall not be lower than the highest point of the withers.

4 The measurement shall be taken at the highest point of the withers.

5 All measurements must be made with all four of the animal's shoes removed.

6 If an official measurer is in any doubt in regard to the measurement of an animal, he should not proceed with the issue of a measurement form until the animal has been jointly measured with another official measurer, in which case the names of both official measurers will appear on the certificate.

7 If an animal on presentation to an official measurer shall in his opinion be unfit for any reason or present evidence of improper preparation, the owner shall be informed that the animal will be measured at a later date, and when it is in a fit

condition to be measured. Where an official measurer takes this course of action, he shall immediately inform the secretary of the Joint Measurement Scheme of his decision, and the name of the animal and of its owner.

8 At the time of measurement, the owner will be required to sign a declaration that to the best of his/her knowledge the animal has not been measured before for a certificate, or if the answer is in the affirmative to give details on the declaration form, which is part 1 of the measurement form to be completed by the official measurer.

NOTE: It is suggested that when making their measurements official measurers should handle the animals quietly and give them reasonable and sufficient time to settle down before taking the measurement.

The name of the official measurer will appear on the measurement certificate.

The societies reserve the right to have any animal remeasured by two referees appointed by the Royal College of Veterinary Surgeons and in the meantime to withdraw the existing certificate.

An objection against a Joint Measurement Scheme certificate may only be lodged at a show, and may only be made by an adult exhibitor who has an animal competing in the class in question, or by the chairman or secretary, on behalf of the show executive, at which the animal is competing. In addition an objection may be lodged by the judge of the class in question through the secretary of the show. In the absence of the exhibitor or in the event of the exhibitor being a minor the objection may be made by their accredited representative.

When an objection is laid at a show against an animal holding a measurement certificate under the scheme, a deposit of ten pounds (£10) must be lodged with the show secretary, who must inform the Secretary, Joint Measurement Scheme, National Equestrian Centre, Kenilworth, Warwicks CV8

2LR, of the action taken, within 24 hours. The show executive will withhold the prize money for the class and forward the certificate of the animal objected to, together with the deposit and any relevant documents, by registered post, to the Secretary, address as above, with the least possible delay. No objection can be entertained unless this procedure is carried out.

1   When an objection has been laid against any animal the address of its permanent stables shall be ascertained by the show secretary at the time the objection is laid or as soon as possible thereafter and he shall notify the Secretary, Joint Measurement Scheme of the said address.

2   No animal in regard to which an objection has been laid may be stabled at any place other than its permanent stables pending re-measurement and the determination of the objection unless the stewards acting in their absolute discretion shall have given their prior approval for such transfer between stables to take place.

3   In the event of any animal in regard to which an objection has been laid being moved to stables other than its permanent stables, without prior approval of the stewards, the objection shall be deemed to have been upheld, without a re-measurement being carried out and the height certificate shall be deemed to be null and void.

4   In the event of a height certificate becoming null and void in terms of the last foregoing sub-rule, the stewards may decline to issue any further height certificate in respect of the said animal for such a period, not exceeding twelve months, as they may decide in their absolute discretion, and shall inform any society in which the animal is registered of any decision taken in this regard.

The Royal College of Veterinary Surgeons have appointed a panel of referees, from which two will be selected to re-measure the animal in dispute. The owner, show secretary and objector will be informed of the referees' decision.

The objector or representative of a society, and the owner or his representative, may be present at the re-measurement, but in no circumstances whatsoever will the re-measurement be delayed due to the absence of the objecting party. The referees may, at their discretion, and for the purposes of the re-measurement, demand that the objector, representative of a society, and/or owner or his representative should leave the area while the re-measurement is being carried out.

The decision of the referees shall be final and binding. In the event of disagreement between two referees, the matter will be reported to the Secretary, National Equestrian Centre, Kenilworth, Warwicks CV8 2LR. The stewards will then decide what course of action is necessary in conjunction with the Royal College of Veterinary Surgeons.

In the event of the animal coming within the height required the ten pounds deposit will be forfeited and the certificate endorsed rendering it immune from further objection, subject to, the conditions as laid down in rules (c) and (d).

In the event of the animal *not* coming within the height required, the deposit will be returned to the person lodging the objection, and the certificate will be duly corrected.

3

How Does One Choose
the Best Arab?

The Arab Horse Show, which takes place each year, is a rendezvous for the lovers of this breed who come from every part of the world to watch the glorious stallions, graceful mares and their progeny of all ages being exhibited, both in-hand and ridden. The first day of the show is given up to pure-bred Arabs and part-bred; Anglo-Arabs play their part on the second. It is usually held towards the end of July, frequently in the grounds of Kempton Park racecourse within easy reach of London.

How does one recognise a good Arab? When watching a class filled with the best animals of this breed parading the ring it is often difficult to decide which in fact has the greatest number of good points. Yet the Arab is so beautiful and so highly individual it should be easy to recognise his qualities providing one looks always for perfection. Weaknesses and bad points cannot be accepted, particularly if they indicate that the horse in question is off-type.

It will help if we discuss the particular qualities which are essential to the true Arabian, and at the same time carefully examine the photographs of leading champions and show-ring winners (pp33-4).

Take first of all the head, of which the forehead must be very broad. The brilliant and remarkably intelligent eyes are circular and large and placed much lower in the skul than those of other horses. They should be prominent, contributing towards the Arab's air of expectancy—he misses little and is quick to sum up any situation. The head itself is small, shorter than that of the average horse, which somehow gives it a finer finish, a special air all its own. Note the delicate, small muzzle and flaring nostrils. Was it this particular feature which caused him to be called 'drinker of the wind'? The profile is concave, not quite straight, and this 'dished' effect is caused by a bulge between the eyes, reaching to a point between the ears and down across the first part of the nasal bone, where there is a slight dip. This is more noticeable with some Arabian horses than with others and is easy to spot in the photograph of the stallion Dargee (see p33).

The jowl is wide and deep and the bars of the mouth longer than is usual in other breeds. There should be quite a width between the jawbones. The small, well-pricked ears turn in and it can be seen from the photograph of Nerinora (see p34) that those of the mare are longer in proportion to her size than those of the stallion.

The neck of the Arabian horse should be strong, full of grace and beautifully proportioned, narrowing near the head but never weak, and becoming wider where it joins the body. The withers are not high but slope into a strong, level back, and they are sometimes broader than those of other horses. The late Lady Wentworth pointed out that the height of the withers has no bearing on the position of the shoulder blade but only on the position for keeping back the saddle.

The hair of the mane and proudly carried tail should be soft and fine—in fact it is often as silky as that of a woman. Another point for the novice judge to remember is that the croup must be flat and long, the tail almost on a level with the top line of the body. A low-set tail and sloping quarters are not correct and definitely off-type. So are ewe necks and general weediness. This is self-evident in all the photographs.

Look, too, for short cannon bones; these are especially noticeable in Dargee (see p33) and Nerinora (see p34). The forearm must be muscular and the elbows should stand well away from the body. Length between the points of hip and buttock, see Darjee, and strong hocks, see Majal (p34), are also important.

It is easy to spot that all the Arabians in the selection of photographs have good shoulders and a pleasing length of rein, proportionate to their size and general make-up. They are superbly made horses with none of the faults which are sometimes masked and indeed overlooked by, for example, a particular elegance or a delightful temperament.

To sum up, in the examples given you will find no weak, narrow shoulders, hocks too bent or too slender for work, weakness across the loins and back, awkwardly made withers or bodies which are either shallow or lacking in depth or too heavy for their owner's legs, or feet which are not hard and round. All is in proportion and framed for efficiency.

When speaking of the judging of a class of stallions Mr R. S. Summerhays, himself a great lover of this breed, reminds us that 'Over all this must be the regal dignity and exquisite grace which are the very essence of the high caste Arabian stallion. No judge should ever forget this or tolerate for one moment the feminine type.'

The second day of the Arab Horse Show is given over to the judging of the Anglo-Arabs and the part-breds.

To put it very simply, the Anglo-Arab originally derived from the crossing of Arab and thoroughbred blood and one or other of these, in the permitted proportions, always appears in its pedigree. The part-bred results from crossing Arab and any non-thoroughbred blood. It may be that the cross consists of a pure-bred Welsh and an Arab, both in their respective studbooks, but the progeny is then part-bred, not Anglo-Arab.

In England an animal is eligible for the Anglo-Arab Stud Book provided it is either a direct cross between a thoroughbred registered in the General Stud Book at Weatherby's and a pure-bred Arabian registered with the Arab Horse Society; or the progeny of such animals; or the progeny of a registered Anglo-Arab and a thoroughbred registered in the General Stud Book or a registered pure-bred Arab.

In the French Anglo-Arab Stud Book the proportion of Arab blood in any youngster seeking registration must never be less than 25 per cent. For example, an Anglo-Arab mare may be put to a thoroughbred stallion, and if she already carries 50 per cent Arab blood in her pedigree this will ensure that there is as much as 25 per cent in her foal. Thus the French Anglo-Arab is a recognised breed composed of Arab, Anglo-Arab and thoroughbred blood. Years ago they were bred in France to a considerable extent and were used largely as remounts for the army. They were also raced and used for show-jumping. Several French horsemen, both in France and at our Royal International Horse Show, have won some important jumping competitions with them. Fortunately there are still a few good studs in France and they are also bred in England to a certain extent. During recent years one of the most outstanding has been Desert Storm (see p71), by Connetable (Anglo-Arab Stud Book) out of Eastern Twilight (General Stud Book). She is now retired to stud after a very fine career in both hack and dressage competitions.

In the part-bred classes on the second day at the Arab Horse

Show some quite famous animals can often be seen, as the Arab has sired not only many champion hacks and delightful riding horses but some remarkably valuable children's ponies. When breeding a foal great care must always be taken to use a good Arabian stallion and not put him to a poor mare or it is unlikely that you will get a youngster worth his keep. It does not matter if you do not know the breeding of your mare as long as she is a nicely proportioned animal who can move well and has a pleasant temperament. Equally a good pony or other non-thoroughbred sire put to a well-made Arab mare may bring very satisfying results. But remember that indiscriminate breeding is a menace.

Another well-run show is the Arab Breeders' Show held at Barrie, Ontario, at which on one occasion Phyllis Hinton was asked to judge the part-bred Arabian classes. She was impressed by the remarkable variety of classes, the superb tack, which had to be entirely correct in events like Half-Bred Arabian Pleasure Horse (Western) and many others, including those for native costume, which have opened up a new world of showing. Thirty horses or more may compete in the ridden classes, and their speed, activity and obedience is remarkable, as are some of the riders' fabulous costumes.

The pure-bred and half-bred Arabians each had their own arenas. She had little opportunity to watch the pure Arabs but there was a large number and at first glance there seemed to be some very nice ones among them. The following is the wording for the class for the Arabian Pleasure Horse (English open) and how it had to be judged:

To be shown at a flat-footed walk on a reasonably loose rein, a collected and an extended trot, a good easy canter and a hand gallop. At the judge's discretion horses shall change from any gait to a flat-footed walk on a loose rein. To be judged on manners, performance, quality and con-

47

formation. No martingale or tie-down.

A steward who knows his job and has a good parade voice is a 'must' in these classes. The horses are not off-saddled or shown in-hand.

There was also the Command Class, which is judged on the responsiveness of the horse to any command of the judge immediately. 'May be asked to stop, turn or change gaits at any time.' A half-mile trotting race, Arabian working hunter, junior equitation, dressage, informal driving and many other performance events were all dealt with on one day, as well as twenty-five breeding classes for pure and half-bred Arabs. Although not always as spectacular as some of the ridden events these breeding classes were intensely interesting and most of them were of fine quality.

Among the half-breds were to be found youngsters who have since made a name for themselves, such as Mrs John Kitchen's Hawthorne Shebarrah, who was three parts Arab and one part pony, and who has been sought after by buyers as far away as Europe. Arab blood seems to be highly respected in Canada and was used—not always wisely—in crossing such widely different animals as Quarter Horses and Shetlands.

In Canada, the United States, Australia, South Africa and of course in various countries in Europe are Arab studs of considerable magnitude and importance. Some have started comparatively recently, others have a long and illustrious history. For many generations the Arab has played a vital part in the life of his desert-bred owner, invoking respect, even veneration. One wonders whether this environment has helped to make him what he is, a creature of fire—noble, intelligent and self-respecting. Physically his surroundings have given him the power to endure, have built in toughness, stamina and speed in relation to his type and size. He has always been spoken of as the friend of man and this is how he seems to regard himself. Indeed the Prophet Mohammed often referred to the Arab horse with feeling and real admiration, and commented on his constant service, his vital assistance in warfare and the fact that 'after woman comes the horse for the enjoyment and happiness of man'.

The Arab may no longer be so essential to life in the Middle East, nor may he receive the love and kind treatment that was once his lot, but fortunately some very fine studs have still remained. One of these is that of His Highness Sheikh Isa Bin Sulman Al Khalifa, ruler of the Bahrain Islands. Here the extremes of climate range from hot and humid to dry and cold but the soil is rich in lime and the water has a high malt, mineral and fluorine content which, combined with a diet of dates, bran, barley and green lucerne all the year round, have helped to create a healthier horse with good bone. No doubt these factors working in conjunction with the principle of the survival of the fittest have combined to keep away the usual diseases and weaknesses and have also contributed to long life and productivity. The same used to, and still should, apply to the ponies of some of our native breeds who lived a free, hard but healthy life.

At the Royal Stud are about 500 Arabians, the stallions varying in height from 14.3hh to as much as 16hh, and the mares from 14.2hh to 15hh. They carry themselves 'with regal and noble bearing yet in stallions and mares alike there is an innate gentleness'. The stallions may each have his own stud of forty mares but the mares are rotated among the stallions to avoid close in-breeding. During the day the mares and foals roam the desert at liberty, returning home at sunset to stand by their feeding troughs and to be attached by the leg to a chain 4ft long. They are never tied by the head, which would be in the nature of an indignity. To accustom both stallions and mares to the chain a thick rope is tied round the pastern of a foreleg when they are youngsters of perhaps six months old. It remains there for a few days.

Some are dark brown at birth, then change to dark grey and become pure white at maturity. Others may be born brown, change to roan and finish up speckled grey; or black at birth turning finally to silver grey. At two years the colts, having already been halter-broken, are taught to stand still when mounted, and to walk, turn and stop. Then they are left free to grow mentally and physically for another year before being further educated.

Arabs will sometimes compare their best horse with a Saluki, which is looked upon as the Arabian greyhound. The mares and Saluki bitches often play together in the desert and the Salukis will never bark nor the mares kick. The Arab horse, whether in England or his native desert, has a remarkable extended trot, but in Bahrain they are not trained or ridden at this gait, which is not found comfortable without a saddle.

In a delightful booklet *The Living Treasures of Bahrain* Danah Al Khalifa declares that:

Stallions not in racing are kept separately, away from the mares, so as to learn good manners in each other's company. They stand, eat and sleep close together, within biting and striking distance. With the exception of playful nips they are perfectly well-mannered. Misbehaviour on a horse's part, when in mixed company, is not tolerated and is corrected with a harsh word, which is sufficient. A true Arab will never thrash his horse.

They are raced but no whips are permitted. Sometimes a hollow bamboo reed is used as it makes a low, whistling sound when waved in the air to encourage the horse to an even greater speed. Incidentally, as well as races for Arabs there

Page 51 (*above*) Sport, one of the most famous cobs of recent years, chosen as Cob of the Year on at least six occasions. He is owned by Mrs Z. S. Clarke and ridden by Mr N. R. Clarke. His body is admirably proportioned, he moves without the slightly carriage-horse action sometimes found in other cobs, and has perfect manners and temperament; (*below*) Turkdean Cerdin, a small cob stallion less than 13.2hh at 4 years old. Bred by Major and Mrs Crotty, he is already a notable winner against strong competition. His head is well set-on to a strong neck, and he is able to flex without difficulty. The neck joins the withers very gracefully and shows to perfection his excellent shoulder, and his short back and quarters give him requisite strength. He is well ribbed up and well coupled, with strong but not coarse limbs, ideal pasterns and feet. Note his good knees and hocks

Page 52 The 1972 Hack of the Year at Wembley, Right Royal, owned by Richard Ramsey and ridden by Vera Holden. He is a true hack and his quality is self-evident

Page 53 The judge, Mrs Nigel Pease, fixes a rosette on Mrs E. Smith's Fiesta Magic, ridden by David Tatlow

Page 54 (*above*) Another Hack of the Year, Moonstrike, ridden by Vanessa de Quincey. Her grace, beauty and delightful temperament, combined with inspired and patient training and riding, made her unique; (*below*) Berrydon Lad, a champion hack, who was trained and presented by Mrs McHugh. He is not as true to hack type as some of his fellow competitors but nevertheless his good looks and way of going brought him success

are also events for pure-bred racing camels who go like the wind.

The following extract from a poem written by Salim Abdulla in the 1860s for the man who was then ruler of Bahrain explains to us in the pleasantest possible fashion how an Arab mare should be appreciated.

Allah hath blessed Bahrain
    in abundance.
And clothed her in finest raiment.
Know ye there existeth a mare
    Swift
With highborne silken tail
Broad and level of croup
With rounded hip and short back
The length of thumb and forefinger;
Not thumb and longfinger.

Her stride swalloweth the distance
Yet her canter becometh
    a soft cushion.
She standeth high over the earth
Deep of girth and
Lean of flank as the bounding saluki
Long is her neck which joineth
A delicate throat
Her large head flexeth with ease
Yea, it is likened unto a rich
    merchant's safe.

How exquisite her ears
Pointed as a date flower bud.
A comely blaze enhanceth her
    smooth cheeks
And generous mouth.

55

And long black lashes
Fringe her great eyes which are
Likened to those of the desert oryx.

Scattered all over Britain today are many large studs of the utmost importance as well as smaller ones of very fine quality, but it seems invidious to describe one without attempting the almost impossible task of mentioning them all—this would take up most of the space in the whole book! But much useful information about them appears in the quarterly magazine *The Arab Horse Society News*, published by the Arab Horse Society (see p188).

4

The Cob: the Handyman of the Horse World

Although for centuries Arabs, hunters and ponies have had a place in literature and have inspired some classic prose and poetry, one cannot recall anything of much importance relating to cobs. It is, however, only fair to mention a poem by one Guto'r Glyn, who lived in the era between 1445 and 1475 and wrote of *Pedigree of a Welsh Cob* in which he refers to a horse whose dam was the daughter of 'the stallion of Anglesey', a redoubtable animal who carried eight people. One wonders if this is the earliest example of poetic licence, or was the cob indeed something out of this world?

It shows a strange lack of appreciation that cobs have not inspired some great artist or writer to immortalise them in oils or water colour or make us conscious of them in the most lovely words and singing phrases of the English language. They have done more than their share of service to man in the past and are indeed great individualists, abounding in common sense, handsome and impressive exponents of the poetry of movement.

Wales is the home of the cob, although they are to be found in the West Country, particularly in parts of Cornwall and the Porlock Area, and in Ireland. Cobs have existed in Wales for many centuries and each crofter had his own Welsh cob mare, but as a rule it is difficult to trace the records of the stallions back for more than about 170 years. These stallions, one of the most famous of which was Comet, included several Flyers with a suitable prefix, True Briton, Brenin Gwalia and many others who helped to create the breed as it is today.

It is rather an interesting fact that a group of Germans visited a fair at Lampeter in 1914 and bought every light horse they could lay hands on, of which almost all must have been cobs, and they also bought every cob they could find in Cardiganshire. This clean-out of livestock must have had a considerable effect on the number of cobs left in Wales and probably had an effect on future breeding.

In judging a cob in an in-hand breed (not ridden) class, whether a stallion, a mare, or young stock of any age, it is wise to stick to the good old-fashioned stamp of animal as far as possible, bearing in mind (especially with regard to stallions and mares) that this is your breeding material for the future.

They should be compact, with a strong back; powerful loins, well laid-back shoulders and withers; depth of girth; noble eye; alert, small ears; quality head; strong, short cannon bone; nice, slightly sloping pastern; the best of feet; and strong quarters, forearm, second thigh and hocks. Any colour is acceptable, except skewbald or piebald. A cob must not be split up behind and must be a straight, free mover, using his knees and hocks well, but not necessarily with too high an action.

The height of the Welsh cob was estimated over the years

at around 15hh but there are many smaller ones of 14hh or
14.2hh and some are bigger, but no particular height limit is
specified now by the Welsh Pony and Cob Society (see p189).
The highly useful pony of cob type must not exceed 13.2hh.
The principles of judging both cob and pony of cob type are
the same, bearing in mind that obviously the pony is lighter as
well as smaller. Usually they are strong, graceful and full of
quality.

The cob which is ridden in the ring at horse shows is not
necessarily bred in Wales but is often the result of surprising
experiments and may contain anything from Percheron to
Arab blood, or indeed thoroughbred or good hunter lines—he
is very much a hybrid. In this case he cannot be registered
with the Welsh Pony and Cob Society although he comes
under the aegis of the British Show Hack and Cob Association (see p188).

When entries were more plentiful than is the case now there
were usually two classes at the big shows, one for those not
exceeding 15.1hh and up to 14st 7lb, and another with the
same height limit but up to more weight than 14st 7lb. Now
there is usually only one event, which is for mares and geldings not exceeding 15.1hh, capable of carrying 14st or over,
or of simply carrying more than 14st.

Except for the fact that piebalds and skewbalds are allowed
in the ridden classes the same rules should apply as for the
breed classes, providing one recognises that the ride the cob
gives the judge counts for a good deal. He is, or should be, well
balanced, able to carry more weight than one which is badly
balanced, even if the latter may be a larger animal. The
correctness of the proportions of his body and limbs and how
they are put together help him to achieve balance. He must
never be shallow, nor must his body be too heavy for his legs.

The true riding cob should not only have quality but be
well-coupled if he is to carry weight, with matching forehand

front and the quarters do not look quite as if they belonged to the same horse? This gives them a most unbalanced appearance. Sometimes, too, they are disproportionately heavy in front or behind.

Your cob must be a cob, not just a smallish, if solid weight-carrying hunter. He needs to be more compact, more powerful for size and use his shoulders to the full, with perhaps a slightly higher action at the gallop. One expects an unreasonable amount from him, as he must have most of the best qualities but none of the faults of the hack and the hunter, plus an individuality all his own, usefully leavened with common sense and patience with his rider—who does not always know best!

The cob must—and usually does—walk out well and trot admirably, but under no circumstances should he be allowed to remember his ancient heritage and trot too fast, bringing to mind the days when he was a very able harness as well as saddle horse. He should oblige the judge with a very pleasant slow canter and gallop on with great verve and dash, although he cannot quite equal the speed of the thoroughbred. He should move fairly lightly in proportion to his size and weight, not 'go into the ground' or pound along too heavily at the gallop unless the going is remarkably hard, or he has been sent on extra fast when carrying a heavy rider. Usually he has plenty of stamina and is very clever on his feet. And these should be good matching feet of dense horn, not small and open at the heel.

His pasterns must be fairly but not disproportionately short, as this is a help when carrying weight over rough, uneven country, and sufficiently sloping to act as springs, to cushion the shock to his joints and limbs and add to the comfort of his rider. If the slope is too acute this obviously constitutes a weakness, as they will receive too much strain. Neither must they be too upright. Most cobs' heads are of noble quality, not too big, with large and kindly eyes set well apart. It is said that since docking became illegal he has lost much of his stylish appearance and special characteristics. But a good cob always looks a good cob, with or without a tail, and if exhibited by a clever rider, as he should be, he cannot fail to catch your eye.

Perhaps one of the most persistent and memorable of champions in ridden cob classes is Mrs Z. S. Clark's Sport (see p51), who enjoys hunting in the winter and showing throughout the season. All show horses and ponies need a change, or, if you prefer, a more natural way of life during the major part of the year, and hunting supplies a thrill and a chance to use their own initiative into the bargain. Without it or some similar distraction they will become bored, then ring crafty, the judge will have difficulty in getting a good ride out of them and down the line they will go.

Comparatively few people realise that boredom and/or excessive repetition are inimical to the good manners and reliable temperament of the average horse or pony. Various small faults begin to appear, both in the stable and when ridden, and these grow into more serious ones which are hard to eradicate.

5

The Graceful Hack:
His Qualities and Training

Graceful, full of quality, completely obedient and delightful
to ride; these are some of the characteristics you may hope to
find in the good hack. He is indeed a pleasure horse and should
add greatly to the dignity of his rider, making him seem a
king among men, more than able to understand and effort-
lessly command the most highly trained and spirited animal.

Up to a point you must look for the same indications of
good conformation and movement in hacks, hunters and
ponies. There are, however, many additional factors to be
considered, dependent on the particular job which each type
of animal will be expected to carry out. This also applies to
performance. The hack must be a beautiful mover in addition to the other qualifications mentioned earlier and not likely
to be readily flustered; ponies must have good manners and
be in every way suitable for their young riders, and hunters

must have almost unlimited scope!

A great deal of the material and suggestions contained in these chapters devoted to different events link up with each other. For example a large part of the training and preparation of the hack is equally suitable for the 14.2hh pony, the hunter, the cob—and the jumper.

The word hack has been given many different meanings and its special significance in connection with the show ring have often been discussed. In our opinion the words of Nimrod, the famous nineteenth-century hunting correspondent, written in 1831 are the most appropriate. He stated that 'Although it is not necessary or to be expected that a hack should be a hunter, yet a hunter to be perfect should be a good hack. The chief paces for a hack to carry a gentleman are the walk and the canter. A very quick trot is a most ungentlemanlike pace, and only fit for a butcher.' Nimrod omitted to mention the possibility of a collected or extended trot, and he was referring to manners and movement, not conformation.

One used to hear about the 'covert hack', a very useful and by no means bad-looking type of horse who may have carried his master to a meet of hounds; in any case to the first covert and possibly to potter about but not do any serious hunting. After writing this description we confirmed it with that of Mr R. S. Summerhays in his *Encyclopaedia for Horsemen* (1962), and we feel that we must add this final comment, which reads 'should also be able to jump in case the hunter fails to arrive at the meet!'

Although a covert hack certainly had to be versatile the show hack of today derives more from the handsome creature who was expected to do credit to his master or mistress when they went for an outing, possibly in Rotten Row. Even in the nineteenth century it was a question of keeping up with the Joneses. There can be little doubt that the pair hack class derives from this fashion, ie a good-looking man, immaculately turned out on an extremely showy riding horse escorting his girl friend of the moment, who cantered slowly beside him in perfect harmony, her ample side-saddle skirt adding grace to the general ensemble and her horse with his flowing mane and tail and satin coat looking gay but completely manageable.

It has been said that at some period during their outing the cavalier would execute a few advanced, or even high school movements to impress his lady—and of course the other on-lookers. In the modern show ring interpretation of this pleasant outing, ie a pair hack class, any such display must be given by both riders.

There is indeed a very real art in riding and presenting a hack in the ring—the right horseman or woman will not only add very considerably to the cash value of a good animal but will do much to cover or mitigate the defects of a one of lesser magnitude.

This is perhaps the right moment to speak of the ladies' hack. First of all there is a certain difference in the judging as the animal must be a comfortable side-saddle ride. A horse which has won the open event does not necessarily win this one, even if he is a very good animal in every other respect.

It is a great advantage to a side-saddle horse to have considerable length of rein—a good shoulder, neck and front—to carry his head well and not be too compact. As the late Mr Horace Smith, a well-known judge and exhibitor in hack classes, once said, 'You don't want the wheels right under you.' He did *not* mean that the horse must be too long in the back; obviously he must have a good back, be well ribbed up, with strong loins. All important points, you may say, and one which should automatically be part of any prizewinner, but there can be a surprising difference between one horse and another when it comes to carrying a side-saddle.

In a ladies' hack or a ladies' hunter class the rider must be turned out well—she must be trim and tidy with her hair neatly netted. And it is most essential that she has been actually taught to ride side-saddle properly or she will spoil both her chances and her horse. Side-saddle riding is both an art and a science. Compare two riders, a good and a bad one. The good one will ride with elegance, sitting straight in the saddle, looking between the horse's ears, both knees to the saddle and her left leg in much the same position as it would be astride. Her horse will move with confidence and when he is standing still she will drop her hand low, thus emphasising the length of rein and his good front. The bad rider, even if she is well turned-out, will look untidy with hands, skirt and legs all flying and probably her body will be slightly crooked. The odds are in this case that the horse will reflect his mistress.

Hacks are not a breed. They are 'discovered', trained and produced in either a novice or an open class, the height limits being, not exceeding 15 hh and exceeding 15 hh, but not exceeding 15.3 hh. Some lean more towards the thoroughbred racehorse, others towards the hunter and others again towards the pony. But the ideal animal is none of these. Unfailingly elegant, he must combine the quality of the racehorse with some of the substance of the hunter but without the raciness of the one and the more solid appearance of the other. He must have a beautiful head, not large but not of pony-type. A good Anglo-Arab can produce these characteristics and we have seen one or two do very well in these events.

An important point to remember is that a horse must go forward with true impulsion in the ring and also that the exhibitor must have good material to work on even if his animal is not as true to type as one would like. In short, it just is not possible to make a silk purse out of a sow's ear. Watch always for free movement of the shoulder at the walk and at the trot. The hind feet should be placed in front of the tracks of the front feet. The good hack must point his toe—and never leave his hocks behind.

The task of the judges is not an easy one. They must look for perfection, in manners, in way of going and in conformation. Classes intended for the horse which must gallop across country such as the hunter seem to have a more definite objective. But in hack classes it can be difficult to find the horse which combines all the requisite qualities in perfect proportion. Because of this the unfortunate judge may have to choose between the best looker and the best-trained animal which is not so well-made. He may have other problems too.

On one occasion a foreign judge was officiating at a big show and he gave the hacks a thorough try out. A really well-educated horse meant everything to him and he caused quite a sensation by awarding first prize to a most worthy animal which gave him the kind of ride he expected but just lacked the glamour of those who usually stood at the top.

Another point which can cause discussion is that the hack is not expected to be a highly trained dressage horse. This is outside his metier and a superb display of training has been described as showing off, or trying to take an unfair advantage. All one can say in this connection is that it is not a requisite of the class—you can win without it. So never imagine that to compete in a hack class is too difficult an undertaking for you.

It is always interesting to observe the well-balanced trot carried out by one or two of the experts who have got their horse on the bit, going as he should. Note the carriage of the head which is just high enough to make it possible for the reins to run almost on level lines to the hands of the rider, and which is also bent at the poll, but never overbent so that the horse's mouth is tucked in near his chest. Observe too, the impulsion of the hocks which are right under him, not trailing behind, the whole giving a wonderful impression of controlled power, obedient to the wishes of the rider and ready and able to carry out with maximum efficiency any movement which may be required.

Later the horse will canter on, demonstrating up to a point the length of his stride, followed by a short display which will indicate his training, obedience and ability. He may be asked to canter a figure-of-eight at a slow, even pace, changing legs perfectly before starting on the second of the two circles. The novice hack, whose training and experience are not so advanced may be steadied to a trot before being asked to change on to another leading leg, but the more experienced animal will execute a flying change, ie change in mid-air at the canter, which is a most graceful movement to watch if correctly executed. It is, however, better to slow down to a trot before changing leg in the figure-of-eight if your hack is likely to bungle it. It is said that the perfect flying change is seldom seen.

He may also show his collected and extended paces, perhaps carry out a half or full pass and he will certainly be asked to rein back. To do this he must first be standing straight on all four legs and move back straight—his legs must move diagonally. He then usually receives a pat as a gesture of appreciation for a brave try and, after standing still for a moment with a loose rein, is allowed to return to his place at the ordinary walk.

These are a few aspects of the correct presentation of the hack, which can be a pleasure to watch, or which may, disappointingly, lack finesse—the final polish which makes all the difference between that which is so rewarding to accomplish or enjoy and the mediocre, which is a boring waste of time.

In addition to the acknowledged methods of getting your horse or pony ready you will have to use your own ingenuity to a certain extent as, no matter what his type, every animal has individual kinks—either physical or mental—which you and you alone will be able to straighten out. This calls for natural aptitude and the ability to learn by experience.

The following hints may be of some practical use to you in preparing your hack for the ring. No time-table has been used in these notes on the general training of a hack, as they are not intended to outline a system of education, but to explain what the hack needs to know in order to put up a good show. We can divide them conveniently into seven sections. They are as follows:

1 *What to teach your hack.* We will assume that you have purchased a nice green four-year-old which will be five next spring. This is a difficult 'teen' age at which the horse has not finished growing either mentally or physically. He is still young and unpredictable to a certain extent. He may have been long-reined, backed and ridden a few times, but has received no consistent training. You need, therefore, to set yourself a definite objective and a steady, progressive schedule.

You will probably have to teach your horse to bridle, to flex his jaw and at the poll, to get his hocks under him, and his weight in the right place, ie not too much on his forehand. You must make sure that he strides out well, that he is equally good both extended and collected, and that he understands the simple aids and is responsive to them.

Many people will say, 'Elementary, my dear Watson'. But can they explain why this initial training or dressage, which should be part of the education of every horse, be he pony or hunter, is so often entirely dispensed with? It is as important a preliminary to the horse as learning to read is to the child.

You must train him to stand to be mounted; to canter on and come back to you easily without throwing his head; to rein back and canter off with the desired leg; to pass to right or to left easily, and to carry out a figure-of-eight.

You may think it is unnecessary for the good hack to be capable of all this. But remember that this training is an extremely useful one, and will help to make him handy under all circumstances. It will develop him, muscle him up, and if properly carried out will please the most captious hack judge. It is certainly not advanced training. Your four-year-old hack must gradually learn, practise and understand all these things until they become an automatic, almost an ineradicable habit. It will take a long time.

If, however, you have purchased an older horse, say a seven-year-old, which you imagine to be in prime of life, you may have to rearrange the curriculum. An over-schooled or sickened horse must forget his trouble. Give him plenty of extended work, and a variety of interests—sometimes a season's hunting will help—before you gradually start re-training him from the very beginning in the simplest possible way. An older horse may have become cunning as a result of bad riding, or lack of education. The best cure is usually to retrain him from the start, as if he had never been broken—probably he never has, in the correct sense of the word; but it is difficult to suggest an antidote without knowing the horse.

Many of the good horses at present on sale have been put into work and into the show ring with little preliminary training. Sometimes they pass into the hands of a novice who takes it for granted that they have been educated, and consequently neither horse nor rider is able to arrive at an understanding; or a dealer who naturally wants to make a quick sale, indulges in a little rough riding or potted schooling which does not inculcate lasting good habits.

Unless you know who trained the horse you decide to purchase you will be well advised to carry out a steady, systematic method of schooling.

2 *Preliminary training.* The first thing to bear in mind is that you cannot train an unfit horse. If he is not in good trim, his muscles tire very quickly, and it is quite impossible to balance him properly. A host of evils ensue, including lying on the bit and boring.

The second and equally important one is that a horse is a creature of habit. Turn this to your own advantage and the training is much more easily carried out. The gradual formation of good habits by slow, steady, absolutely regular daily school work will bring its inevitable reward—a trained, fit horse. Spasmodic schooling will ruin him.

The position in which your hack carries his head is of vital importance. Raising the head lightens the forehand, but if the head is held too low there is often too much weight on the forehand. Unless the horse is well-balanced, an equal distribution of weight, your best efforts will be of little value.

It is to be hoped that plenty of lungeing with two reins, and to either hand, has been carried out as an essential part of your animal's education. This is a specialist's job, and should never be attempted by a beginner on a young horse. It can be practised and gradually learnt on an old school horse, under expert and practical instruction.

Lungeing with the rein attached to the front of the cavesson is sometimes a help but no rule can be made as many horses go far better with it behind. When carrying out lungeing it is advisable to pivot in the centre of your manège keeping your horse exactly between the rein in one hand, the whip in the other. Remember to change direction frequently; do not keep him circling too long on one leading fore leg as this is most tiring to a young horse.

Correct leg work, a light play on the snaffle and the proper use of the bit will help to raise his head and lighten his forehand. Before concentrating on the leg and thigh work, which will help to get your hack balanced, make sure that he understands what you are trying to tell him, that he has been trained to answer to the leg to a certain extent.

The combination of the hands, leg and voice in perfect timing will help him considerably—it takes a good horseman to achieve this precision, and a disjointed effort will do an immense amount of harm. Firm pressure of the leg just behind the girth at the right moment, but under no circumstances a continuous pincer movement or exaggerated kicking, is indi-

Page 71 (*above*) Desert Storm, a registered Anglo-Arab, whose graceful and correct proportions, perfect movement and delightful temperament brought her many championships in hack classes. Owned by the late Miss A. Stubbings, she was trained by the Bullen family and always ridden by Jennie (Mrs Loriston Clarke); (*below*) Col Alois Podhajsky, formerly director of the Spanish Riding School in Vienna, riding the late Mrs V. D. S. Williams's Forty Winks during a schooling exercise

Page 72 (*above*) Sheila Waddington riding Grace and Favour. She won the Badminton Horse Trials on three occasions, and Little Badminton once. Mrs Waddington demonstrates in a natural manner balance and control of her horse—her objective is true collection; (*below*) Henry Gilhuys riding Harta Von Budapest, a 12-year-old grey stallion, bred at the National Stud in Hungary

Page 73 (*above*) The 1972 Hunter of the Year, Mr R. A. Bonett's 7-year-old Admiral, ridden by Roy Trigg—a superb heavyweight; (*below*) Orator, one-time reserve heavyweight champion at Dublin, carrying Mr Dorian Williams, Master of the Whaddon Chase Foxhounds

Page 74 This charming hunter mare, Prince's Grace, ridden by her owner, Mrs A. L. Wood, won brilliantly in ridden show hunter classes. She was always an excellent performer to hounds and has continued her career by achieving many championships as a hunter brood mare

cated; and a long whip, or two canes, lightly applied in conjunction with each leg will quickly make him sensitive to the leg, and to the voice, too.

As regards the use of your hands in collecting your horse, it is essential to give plenty of loose rein work during the preliminary stages, until your horse is fit and ready for greater concentration. Make sure that he understands the uses of the bit in his mouth before expecting too quick a reaction from him.

Hold your snaffle reins in one hand before beginning the light movement on it which will raise his head. The bit should be brought into play as it is needed in conjunction with the snaffle, but great care must be taken not to over-bend the animal by careless use of the curb. It is as well to continue this work with the reins in two hands, but the snaffle and bit reins divided from one another by the four fingers of each hand.

Get your horse's hocks under him and the weight off his forehand—this cannot be stressed too often. And make sure that the most important part of this work is carried out by your legs and thighs in bringing the hocks into action. Your hands support, restrain, inform—they must never be used for haulage purposes.

3 *Pass and half pass*. It is essential that the half pass and the pass should be taught early in the education of your hack, as they will help him immensely in his work. The pass should be taught in small doses. If you have no covered school or outdoor manège try to mark out a track, oblong for preference, or make use of a small field. The hedge or wall will help your horse to perform his first few steps in the pass if you accustom him to it gradually—ask a few steps while you are practising a diagonal change of hand and when you are about to make the change from left to right or vice versa. Two or three side paces at a time is the most you should ask to begin with.

75

Teach the pass by means of the diagonal (right hand, left leg and vice versa) aids: you will have a far better balanced horse than if you use the lateral aids; and make sure that he is collected and making the most of himself at walk or trot before you ask him to begin the half pass. It is best to start with the half rather than the full pass, as it involves less interference with the horse's impulsion—it will be an easier and more natural movement for him.

His head should be slightly bent, from the poll, in the direction which you wish to go, and in answer to the feel of the reins; the opposite or supporting rein will help to hold him straight. Pressure from the opposite leg is applied.

Once the horse really understands your intention this exercise can be practised anywhere, during an ordinary ride for example, and the more often the better. (Remember that he should cross one foot cleanly in front of the other.) Instant obedience is the keynote and the horse should change readily from side to side directly he receives the intimation; a few paces each way are sufficient when you are using it as an obedience test. It is an exercise which will make him supple and handy besides muscling him up.

4 *Flexions.* Does your hack flex easily? Does he understand the flexions, and is he at all times ready with his responses?

In the direct flexion the horse gives his lower jaw and brings his head slightly inwards—it is important to stress the word 'slightly'—bending from just behind the poll. The lateral flexion should cause him to turn his head sideways in addition to relaxing his jaw, but in both cases the body must be kept straight, and he must go well into his bit. The necessity of getting the animal's head into the right place was emphasised in the last section. Until this has been carried out one should not begin to teach the flexions.

The first steps necessary to the teaching of the flexions give a very definite example of the objects and proper use of the snaffle and bit at all times; ie that the snaffle should raise the head, the curb or bit slightly lower it and bring it in. The correct handling of the two, always in conjunction with the legs, is the only road to proper collection.

Direct flexion is usually, though not always, taught from the ground in the first instance. By bringing the snaffle reins over the horse's head and holding them in one hand in front of his nose and about six inches above it, you can indicate to the horse that he is to go forward and to raise his head; while at the same time you feel the bit reins in the other hand, and gently persuade him to flex, to relax his jaw without lowering his head or stopping.

It is of great importance to teach your hack to answer the reins in this way—to respond to these two separate and apparently contradictory instructions. At the first few signs of relaxation the dawning comprehension and co-operation of your pupil should be instantly rewarded. There is no doubt that immediate encouragement and appreciation have the effect of impressing the lesson on the horse, who is likely to remember it more distinctly and be readier to respond in future.

It is easy to come to the conclusion that your hack has a hard mouth because he carries his head in the wrong place and because he is heavy in hand. Get his head right and you will probably find that his responses are better.

Great care must be taken to see that the head is bent from just behind the poll. There is good reason for this maxim— we must raise the neck from below, upwards and not from front to rear as is sometimes done; and if we go about this the wrong way, not only do we fail to distribute the horse's weight properly, but he does not receive the instruction that we intend via the reins.

An over-bent hack, bent from lower down the neck and not from just behind the poll, is never properly collected and pressure on the bit produces the wrong reactions. Collection is not purposeless interference—it brings about the right distribution of weight and makes it possible for the rider to direct the power and propulsion which is 'collected' beneath him and which can be used in a variety of ways.

When the direct flexions are effortless and your hack has made good progress in ordinary straightforward work and changes of direction, you can teach him the lateral flexion, but not until he is obedient and ready for it.

To make the lateral flexion to the left, stand near the off shoulder, and bring the snaffle reins over the horse's head in exactly the same way as for the first instruction in the direct flexion. Hold the snaffle reins in your right hand and the bit reins in your left. Carry out the direct flexion, then lightly push the horse's head to the left with the snaffle reins held high.

The left hand with the curb reins is moved to the left, automatically tightening the left rein—the jaws must give in the sideways flexion as in a direct flexion. Great patience is needed. The neck, while flexing at the poll, must be bent to one side, but the horse must still stand straight. It is a good principle to carry out the lateral flexion at a standstill only during the dismounted lessons, and only while going forward when mounted. You will find that the work is carried out more easily and with less displacement.

At first glance the lateral flexion may seem unimportant, but if you are successful in teaching it to your animal you will have helped considerably towards making him supple and easily co-ordinated in all his movements and ready to obey your instructions. You will certainly make him a great deal lighter in his change of directions. An almost infinitesimal lateral flexion suffices to do this—an exaggerated one is most harmful.

5 *Figure-of-eight.* The value and importance of the figure-

of-eight are not always appreciated. Some people consider that it is elementary and that they can learn to carry it out successfully before they are efficient horsemen in other ways; others appreciate that there are not many riders who can perform it to perfection.

Let us consider the training which produces the animal capable of performing a polished figure-of-eight, and which must be put in hand before the figure eight is attempted. One will assume that he had been taught the necessary preliminaries, consisting of plenty of straightforward work, of circling to either rein, of halting and of the flexions.

The hack which flexes well does not just relax his jaw in answer to his rider's demands—there is far more to it than that. The lateral flexion means the co-ordination of forces, the flexion, or shall we say the giving of the whole side of the body which is under command.

Therefore before attempting to teach the figure-of-eight, which is a flowing movement necessitating balance and effortless performance and which presupposes good discipline and training, make sure that your hack has not only done plenty of work to either rein, but that he understands the shoulder in and shoulder out of the riding school and carries out the full and half pass adequately.

Before starting on the figure-of-eight make sure that your horse will break into a canter on whichever leading leg you choose. Trot round your field or marked track, and as you make the correct turn at the end apply the aids to bring him on to the correct leading leg—if you are on the left rein and wish to lead on the near fore and hind, then turn his head slightly to the left and close both legs, with the emphasis on the right leg, which should be brought slightly further back.

If he obeys correctly make much of him, then canter on, pull back to the trot and repeat the lesson a few times. If he has made a mistake stop and restart immediately, patting him

79

directly he gets it right. Practice this until your horse will obey you at all times, both on the turn and the straight. The necessity for turning his head slightly to the side on which you wish to lead will then be at an end.

Unless you have an exceptionally good sense of direction, or are able to work in a covered school, it is advisable to mark out a nicely proportioned figure-of-eight in whitening before attempting to introduce your horse to this exercise. If it is not possible to use the whitening, a few sticks or stones to define the angles is better than nothing.

Walk, then trot your figure-of-eight to accustom yourself and your horse to it. Then make sure that your animal is comfortably collected, strike off at an angle on the correct leg, and canter the first circle. The angle flows into the circle and the applied pressure of the leg ensures that the horse's quarters are not thrown out of alignment, that his hind feet follow the line of his front feet.

The completion of your first circle and the beginning of the next automatically bring you on a straight line for a few strides, and this is the point at which you change leg. To begin with, in fact for quite a while, it is better to bring your hack back to a trot as you complete the circle, and then put him on the correct leg for the beginning of the next one.

You should be able to feel, to know which leg is leading without looking down. This habit can be easily acquired by the simple practice of closing your eyes when out hacking on a schooled horse and relying on your muscles to tell you on which leg he breaks into a canter, but do not experiment with the young horse during his actual hours of training. Be careful never to look down when changing leg in the show ring, as this will throw you, and therefore your horse out of balance.

The famous flying change or change in the air must not be attempted until you are certain that your horse's obedience to the aids is automatic to the extent that he can even be relied upon to obey the contra aids. Gradually shorten the number of paces which you trot between circles; and make sure that you ask your horse to change at the psychological moment when it is easiest for him to do so.

Use diagonal aids. If your change is from near to off, close both legs, using the left one with greater strength, and feel your right rein, but do not move your hands to the right. The change should be asked just before the horse is about to make his next stride, not when he has just started one. This is where your sense of timing, your being at one with your mount is so important.

It is as difficult to describe this movement as it is to describe the rhythm of perfect dancing. It is sufficient to say that if you and your hack are both disciplined, collected and in unison, you will be able to ask the change without fear of disturbing the centre of balance, or noticeably losing ground. Unless these conditions are fulfilled you will be wise to content yourself with breaking back into a trot for two or three paces between the circles.

Preliminary to the change in the air, the exercise of starting your horse on, let us say, the off fore, stopping and immediately restarting on the near fore should be carried out continuously. This change of leg is obviously helped by the halt. Insistence that the animal shall restart on the opposite leg leads up to the actual moment when the change can be carried out without the halt, and 'in the air'.

6 *Conditioning.* Training is one-third of the battle towards success—conditioning which covers feeding, strapping and trimming and proper presentation in the ring are the other important factors.

It is impossible to lay down hard and fast rules about feeding as some horses are much better doers than others, and it is not always easy to obtain the right food.

The main principles, however, remain the same. Your horse

must have plenty to drink, variety in his diet, be left alone while he is feeding and have four feeds—the first really early, the fourth as late as possible. You can use your ingenuity and imagination in a hundred different ways to produce a balanced diet. Do not disdain rock salt, carrots and linseed.

Make sure that your animal has plenty of air, but is not in a draught or cold. Many horses quickly lose condition which could have been saved by an extra rug. See that he is occasionally treated for worms, and that his teeth do not need filing. Linseed or cod liver oil in his daily feed is often very helpful.

Get your hack fit so that he is in a condition to stand up to a hard day's work without showing signs of distress. See that plenty of time every day is given to strapping and massaging. Beat him up well, but cleverly, with a hay wisp. Spend a long time brushing but not combing, his mane and tail. Pay plenty of attention to his feet.

When you plait his mane on the day of the show—seven plaits is a good number—stitch it firmly, but do not pull it too tight. Put his tail in a bag as well as using a tail guard, if you are travelling by rail or motor horse-box.

7 *Début in the ring.* With few exceptions it is best to ride your hack quietly about for half an hour or more before it is time to enter the show ring, in order to get him accustomed to his surroundings and take off any freshness. Furthermore, you will probably settle down better yourself if you do this, and any minor adjustments to saddle or bridle can be carried out if necessary, although naturally all this should have been checked before you left home.

On the other hand, a few horses are inclined to get into a nervous sweat in anticipation of the ring. This is a habit which they will sometimes lose in the course of time; but it may be necessary to take them straight out of the box and into the class, when quite possibly they will never turn a hair.

Let your hack walk freely round the ring, displaying his length of stride and natural balance. If you have schooled him properly in the first place and his conformation is right this should be an agreeable display of a well-balanced horse at liberty, but ready for obedience and collection; attentive, not sloppy or mischievous.

Do not bunch. There is no occasion to keep behind the animal in front of you; pass it by all means, move freely, provided you do not interfere with your fellow competitors. When you are asked to trot on put your horse into a nicely balanced trot. It is important that your hack points his toe well in the trot; a good swinging trot with sufficient length of stride, steady, and not too fast, will attract the judge's attention far quicker than many more dubious methods.

Talk to your novice hack if he lacks ring experience; your voice will give him confidence, curb his exuberance, and probably help you, too. You will both co-operate the better for it. And a man who talks to his mount is often much less rigid than one who does not.

A 'nice slow canter' is a delight to the eye, but it is not as close an analogy to a ride on a rocking horse as it sounds. Certainly the action should be easy and fluent, and there is no need to hold your horse on a tight rein. But he must go well up into his bridle, be ready and prepared for the slightest indication from you, and the rein should not be slack. If it is, your horse is behind his bridle—he is not a trained hack, or you are an imperceptive and untrained horseman.

The animal which is behind his bridle and the one which pokes his nose are equally objectionable. Very often both faults are the result of insufficient impulsion, and indicate that the strong leg and thigh work so essential a part of good training, have been scamped.

There is one point which cannot be overlooked. The hack, almost more than other horses, must be groomed for stardom, must be turned out looking worth a million dollars, shining with well-being. And he must have that indefinable presence which seems to be born in some animals or may eventually arise from a certain confidence and self-pride. Horses are curiously psychic and sometimes sense these very qualities in their rider.

Here are a few tips: the water marks which look so attractive on the quarters of a hack, in the shape of diamonds or squares, are made by brushing the coat in different directions with a damp water brush. The coat must be fine and silky, but that should not be any problem in the case of a hack.

Imagine a chess board which covers the flat part on the top of the quarters on either side of the spine. Brush the coat in the direction in which it grows, on top of the quarters towards the rear. Then place the point of the brush against the spine and draw it down in a straight line towards the ground, filling in the space with these strokes, each with the width of the brush apart. In the same way draw equally spaced lines from the loins to the rear. You will then have a series of squares the width of the brush in size. All lines running in the same direction must be parallel or the pattern will be very untidy. Take care that the brush is not too wet or the hair will crinkle. To emphasise the width of the lower part of the quarter it is a good idea when you have completed the pattern, to brush the hair below it downwards to a line level with the stifle, then horizontally down to the hock.

The tail should hang level with the hocks when the horse is in action. The easiest way to get it the right length is to cut it about four inches below the hocks or put an arm underneath it and raise it to what is apparently the correct height. It should be full at the bottom but thinned at the top—about twelve inches. The tail helps to balance the horse and is a much-needed protection from flies and from cold winds in the winter. The fly muscles which cause the skin to twitch do not extend round the hindquarters and therefore the tail is the only protection.

When pulling a tail, which must never be cut at the top or it will look like a bottle brush, commence at the top and work downwards on either side, taking out only one or two hairs at a time. Always pull from underneath and never pull out tufts of hair, which would be painful and make the dock sore. Do it gradually, if there is much to be done, taking out only a few hairs a day. You can twist the hair round a comb and give a sharp pull, or use your fingers. Sometimes it helps to ask someone to back the horse against the stable door, hold him still hang his tail over the door and work from outside. Bandage the tail, not too tightly and tie at the bottom; again do not make it too tight, and bend the tail when you have finished to make sure it is comfortable.

You may have noticed that horses' tails are sometimes plaited. Strands of hair are taken from the other side and plaited to form a long plait down the centre and the end of the plait is usually turned under. The plait is about the same length as the thinning would be, about twelve inches, and of course the lower part of the tail is left full.

Practice is required if you are to make a success of any of these jobs and I would suggest that you try to make the water marks (squares and diamonds) at your leisure, without the horse. Stretch a large piece of velvet tightly across a board, equip yourself with a water brush and make a few experiments. You will then be better able to cope with a living model!

6

The Well-Trained Horse: Dressage and What It's All About

Dressage is so much a part of our lives today that it no longer requires much explanation but it seems to us that many people misunderstand its importance. It is primarily intended to educate the horse, make him understand what is required of him and teach him obedience; to make him supple, well-balanced and able to carry out his work with the maximum of efficiency and enjoyment to the man, woman or child on his back and to himself.

Obviously his rider also requires some education before he can be expected to convey his orders to the horse with any degree of skill; a bad rider can confuse and annoy his partner. But there is no mystique or difficulty about simple dressage to anyone who has taken the trouble to learn to ride properly. The

Australian rider, Bill Roycroft, who has competed on various occasions at Badminton and was a member of the Australian team which was fourth in the three-day event at the Olympic Games in Munich in 1972, never had a lesson in dressage. A natural horseman, he studied very carefully and learnt all he knew from good books, of which there are a number. At Munich he had only 36 penalty points in the dressage with his horse Warrathoola, finishing the three days with a bonus score of plus 29.60.

A good training and ability to acquire as few penalties as possible is a 'must' when competing in horse trials, as the idea that an effective speed and endurance test on the second day will make up for bad dressage marks is a fallacy. Another reason for conserving these marks is that if you already have a passable test 'in the bag' it is not necessary to take risks by pressing on too much at the wrong moment in order to gain bonus marks for time on the second day.

You will see dressage carried out in tests at horse shows, in combined training events, and in the three-day horse trials, in which horse and rider give proof of their ability in dressage, speed and endurance (including a steeplechase course and riding across country) and show-jumping. But one must not get the idea that dressage is simply a competitive event. It is not. Basically it is intended for training the horse and it has been used in this manner for many generations.

It is true that the actual term was little spoken of, or that many dressage tests were carried out, in Britain in the 1920s and early 30s but this type of training was used by our leading horsemen. On one occasion John Nestle attended a dressage competition with a horse dealer of the old school who had never had any practical experience of dressage. After he had seen a couple of the competitors carrying out the test John asked him what he thought of it, to which he replied: 'I can't see that it can do any positive 'arm to the 'osses!'

Dressage—or call it training if you like—is required before the hack, the show-jumper or the high-school horse start on their respective careers. Consider the swift twists and turns which are essentially a part of almost any course in an enclosed area such as a stadium. The horse must be as supple as a riding whip and this and other qualities are only achieved with simple dressage. Riding on a circle, gradually reducing the circle in size without making it too small will help in this and other ways (including the positioning of the head and neck), providing the rider makes sure that the horse is bent in the direction in which it is going.

Polo ponies must be able to twist and turn at considerable speed during the game and also to stop in a flash. They must be able to change leg or turn on the haunches with ease. Very often a hunter collects himself when he is going to jump a difficult obstacle, otherwise it is unlikely that he would negotiate it safely.

During recent years some racehorse trainers have found that a difficult horse will react more easily and become a better ride for his jockey in a race if he has had a little elementary dressage.

To sum up, if you are riding along on a loose rein, without contact and you attempt to collect your horse by closing your legs to bring his hocks under him and tighten your reins sufficiently to convey your wishes and control his forehand, this is the beginning of simple dressage.

If you study the following explanations of the various terms used you will be able to enjoy, comment upon and possibly criticise the performances of the various tests. Our apologies to those readers who already have them at their finger-tips and are expecting a more advanced commentary.

First of all, here are some movements which are used in training but not listed precisely by the Fédération Equestre Internationale:

The walk on the long rein. This is a pace between the ordinary and extended walk before the latter can be expected. A nice free, easy walk is required, contact with the reins being maintained.

The strong trot. This is a pace between the ordinary and the extended trot to be executed before the horse is sufficiently trained to be asked a correct extended trot, ie before the training has reached a sufficiently advanced stage to produce the impulsion of the hind legs necessary for the extended trot.

The strong canter. The same as for the trot.

Turn on the forehand. In the turn on the forehand, the horse's quarters are moved in even, quiet regular steps round the inner foreleg. The horse's head must remain in the correct position, the inner foreleg, acting as a pivot, should remain as nearly as possible on the same spot. This exercise must only be done from the halt.

Turn on the haunches. In the turn on the haunches, the horse's forehand is moved in even, quiet and regular steps round the horse's inner hind leg. The inner hind leg, acting as a pivot, should remain as nearly as possible on the same spot. This movement may be done from the halt or from the move. When done from the walk the movement is executed in the same manner as above, but without any definite halt; the horse is taken fluently from the walk into the turn on the haunches.

When done from the trot or from the canter, the pace must be reduced to a walk, the horse taken instantly and fluently into a turn on the haunches and the original pace resumed immediately on completion of the turn.

(The pirouette is a high-school movement, but it should be noted that the difference between the turn on the haunches and the pirouette is that in the pirouette the exact cadence and regularity of movement of whatever pace it is being performed at must be maintained.)

NOTE: A full turn is a turn of 360°; a half turn is a turn

of 180°; a quarter turn is a turn of 90°.

Shoulder-in. In the shoulder-in the horse's quarters follow a straight track parallel to the wall (or direction of movement) while his shoulders, head and neck are bent inwards around the rider's inside leg and flexed in opposition to the movement. The tracks of the forelegs are inside those of the hind legs.

Diagonal. The near-hind and off-forelegs of the horse are known as the right diagonal; the off-hind and near fore as the left diagonal. A rider is said to be riding on the right diagonal when, at the rising trot, his seat returns to the saddle as the horse's near-hind and off-fore come to the ground, and vice-versa. The rider should change the diagonal at every change of direction. It is optional whether he rides on the inside or the outside diagonal, but must conform to the same one throughout.

Counter-lead or false canter. A horse is said to canter false or at the counter-lead when he is made to do a circular movement to the right with the near-fore leading, or to the left with the off-fore leading.

The counter-lead or false canter should not be confused with the disunited canter, in which the horse's leading hind leg appears to be on the opposite side to his leading foreleg.

Simple change of leg at the canter. A simple change of leg at the canter is a change preceded by a half-halt, whereby the horse is brought back into a trot or a walk, restarting from either pace into a canter with the other leg leading.

The following movements are better known. You may observe that several of the terms used in dressage derive from the ballet. Full and precise details of these movements as well as other relevant information are available from the British Horse Society (see p188). The booklet containing this information is: *Dressage Rules and Official Procedure for Dressage Competitions.* Diagrams and details of the various tests can

Page 91 (*above*) A typical middleweight hunter, Mr W. F. Ransom's Spey
Cast, ridden by Jack Gittins. Note his excellent limbs, strong hocks and good
bone, all in proportion and well able to carry his powerful body; (*below*) a
famous hunter sire, the premium stallion Solon Morn (sire Solonaway by
Solferno, dam Hunting Morn by Foxhunter)

Page 92 A trio of ponies. Prosperity of Catherston (*left*) at 6 years old after winning the class for ponies not exceeding 14.2 and the championship at the Royal International Horse Show; (*centre*) the second prizewinner in the same class and the reserve champion, Creden Lucky Charm, exhibited by Graham Rolf; (*right*) Jenny Wren, third in the class and championship, owned by Mr A. Deptford

Page 93 Whalton Caprice, ridden by Carol Scott and owned by Dr and Mrs Gilbert Scott, was consistently successful. Note the good forearm, second thigh and nice length of rein, and admire the well-executed diamond marks on the quarters (see Chapter 5)

Page 94 (*above*) Sinton Samite (sire Bwlch Hill Wind, dam Criban Schiffon), champion brood mare at the 1972 National Pony Show when aged seven and owned by Miss Hind. Note her depth of girth and length of rein; (*below*) one of our most famous pony stallions Bwlch Valentino, whose stock is known throughout the world

also be obtained.

Special conditions. At the halt, and at all movements, the horse must be on the bit. A horse is said to be on the bit when the hock action is correct, the neck is more or less raised according to the speed of the pace, the head is kept quiet, the contact with the mouth is light and no resistance to the rider is offered.

Halt. The horse should stand motionless and straight on all four legs and be ready to move forward at the slightest pressure of the rider's legs. The halt signifies the manner of stopping the horse at the end of a movement and is obtained by a displacement of the weight on the quarters by the action of the seat and by a resisting action of the hand, causing an instantaneous but not abrupt stop, while the legs are kept in readiness to maintain the impulsion.

The half halt is an almost simultaneous action of the hand, the seat and the legs of the rider with the object of increasing the attention and balance of the horse before the execution of several movements or transitions to lesser paces. In shifting more weight on the quarters, the engagement of the hind legs and balance on the haunches are facilitated.

Ordinary walk. A free, regular and unconstrained walk of moderate speed. The horse should walk briskly but calmly, with even and resolute steps, distinctly marking four equally spaced beats. The rider should keep a light and steady contact with the mouth.

When the four beats are not well marked, even and regular, the walk is disunited. The *disunited walk* should not be confused with the amble.

Amble. A pace at which the horse moves his lateral legs simultaneously.

Extended walk. The horse should cover as much ground as quickly as possible without haste or breaking the regularity of the beats. The hind feet pass clearly beyond the tracks of the fore feet. The rider lets the horse stretch out his head and neck

95

F

by extending the reins *without losing contact* so as to be able at any moment to make the horse change his pace and speed or direction.

The free walk on a loose rein serves the purpose of giving the horse a rest, allowing him complete freedom of the head and neck.

Collected walk. The horse should move resolutely forward with his neck raised and arched. The head approaches the vertical position. The hind legs are engaged, ie brought well forward under the body. The pace remains a walk with the normal succession of beats. The collected walk is slightly slower than the ordinary walk, each step covering less ground, but being more elevated owing to the fact that the joints are more bent. The mobility is, therefore, greater without the steps being hurried.

Ordinary trot (natural or utility). This is a pace between the extended and the collected trot. The horse should move freely and quite straight with a balanced and unconstrained bearing, the haunches being very active and well engaged and the contact with the mouth being light. The steps should be as even as possible and the hind legs should follow exactly the tracks of the forelegs.

Extended trot. The steps should be extended, the impulsion of the quarters making the horse use his shoulders energetically. The neck should be stretched out more than at the ordinary trot.

Collected trot. The neck should be raised, permitting the shoulders to move with greater ease in all directions, the hind legs being well engaged and maintaining the energetic impulsion, notwithstanding the slower movement. The steps of the horse are shorter but he is more mobile and light.

The ordinary trot and extended trot should generally be executed rising ('à l'anglaise). The collected trot and slow trot should be executed sitting ('à la française').

Ordinary canter. This is a pace between the extended canter and the collected canter. The horse should be perfectly straight from the poll to the tail and move freely being naturally balanced.

Extended canter. The horse's neck and head are stretched out more than at the ordinary canter. The horse should increase the length of the strides without losing his calmness and lightness.

Collected canter. The horse's shoulders, being unconstrained, should be free and mobile, and his haunches should be active and vibrant. The muscles should be more relaxed without the impulsion being diminished.

Slow trot and slow canter. These paces are less active and their cadence slower than is the case at the ordinary trot and canter. The quarters are higher and less active than at the collected trot and canter.

Change of legs at the canter. This should be executed 'In the air' in a single stride at the moment of suspension. The horse must remain straight, calm and light.

Rein back. This is the walk backwards. The horse must move his diagonal legs simultaneously (by pairs in two-time) back step by step, the haunches remaining well in line, and must be ever ready, at the wish of the rider, to halt or to advance without halting.

At all paces, a slight champing of the bit, without nervousness, is a criterion of the obedience of the horse and the harmonious distribution of his forces. The grinding of the teeth and the swishing of the tail are manifestations of resistance on the part of the horse. The judges must take these into account in their marking.

Change of pace and speed. Such a change should always be distinct but smooth. The cadence of a pace should be maintained up to the moment the pace is changed or the horse halts.

In changing from the rein back to the forward movement the horse should do so without halting.

Change of direction. The horse should adjust the bend of his body to that of the curved line he is tracing.

Work on two tracks. In this exercise the horse moves on two tracks. The head, neck and shoulders must always be in advance of the quarters. A very slight bend permitting the horse to look in the direction of the movement adds to his grace and gives more freedom of movement to the outside shoulder. The outside legs pass and cross in front of the inside legs. There must be no reduction in the pace. The legs on the side to which the horse is moving are the inside legs; those on the opposite side the outside legs.

Work on two tracks can be demanded as follows:

1 Half pass on the diagonal across the arena, in which case the horse remains parallel to the long side ('walls') of the arena.

2 Head to the wall (travers). Quarters to the inside.

3 Tail to the wall (renvers). Quarters to the outside.

The last two movements may be executed on a straight line (along the wall), on a circle or on a volte (small circle).

Serpentine. The first loop is started by moving gradually away from the short side of the arena and the last loop is finished by moving gradually towards the opposite short side.

Counter-change of hand. The horse changes his direction by moving obliquely either to the quarter line or to the centre line or to one of long sides of the arena, from where he returns obliquely to the line of direction followed when starting the counter-change of hand.

Counter-change of hand on two track (zig-zag). The attention of the judges should be concentrated on the changing of the bend of the horse, the crossing of his legs, and the precision, smoothness and regularity of his movements.

When a specified number of steps or strides to either side

is stipulated in the programme of the test, this number must be strictly adhered to.

Any jerky movement at the moment of changing the direction is considered a fault.

Demi-pirouette. This is the half-turn (or turn about) on the haunches. Tracing a half-circle round the haunches, the forehand commences the half-turn, without halting, at the moment the inside leg ceases its forward movement. The horse moves forward again, without halting, upon completion of the half-turn.

Pirouette. This movement is a volte (small circle) on two tracks, the forehand tracing a circle round the haunches and the radius of the volte being equal to the length of the horse.

At whatever pace the pirouette is executed, the horse should turn smoothly, maintaining the exact cadence and regularity of movement of that pace. At the pirouette, as well as at the demi-pirouette, the forelegs and the outside hind leg move round the inside hind leg which forms the pivot and should move on the same spot. At the walk the horse may pivot on his hind leg without raising it off the ground.

Passage. This is a slow, shortened, very elevated and very cadenced trot. It is characterised by the more accentuated bend of the knees and hocks and by the graceful elasticity of the movement. Each diagonal pair of legs is raised and put to the ground alternately, gaining little ground and with an even cadence and a prolonged moment of suspension.

The toe of the raised foreleg should, in principle, reach the height of the middle of the shin of the other foreleg. The toe of the raised hind leg should reach the height only a little above the fetlock joint of the other hind leg.

The same passage cannot be expected of all horses. According to conformation and temperament, as well as energy, some horses have a more rounded and wider action, others a more animated and shorter action. Swaying of the hind quarters is, however, considered a fault.

Piaffer. The passage on the spot without any movement forward, backwards or sideways. If the horse does not remain exactly on the spot, but advances a few centimetres only at each step, the cadence, however, being well marked, regular and brilliant, then the piaffer can be considered no more than *sufficient*, ie obtain no more than half marks for this movement.

All the movements should be executed without any apparent aids from the rider, who should sit erect in the saddle with the loins and hips supple, the thighs and legs steady and the upper part of the body easy, free and straight.

You may have noticed that the judges of dressage competitions are always carefully positioned at the end of the arena, exactly opposite where the competitors enter it. This is the only place from which a test can be properly assessed.

Dressage judges will always look for correctness and regularity and balance in work on two tracks; and also the regularity of a circle and the flexion of the horse. Regularity in all movements is essential. So is a good transition from one pace to another, which must be smooth and seemingly effortless.

Colonel Alois Podhajsky, for many years Principal of the Spanish Riding School of Vienna, describes a good transition to perfection, pointing out that 'The horse should maintain the same rhythm and cadence of movement, only lengthening and shortening the stride at whatever pace he goes. What a pleasure it is to watch transitions performed in such a manner! At the same time they show that the horse is absolutely smooth, supple and well-balanced.'

The Prix Caprilli, originally looked upon as an important dressage test is now also known under another name—the Prix Caprilli Riding Test. It is a test of the rider not the horse, in fact it is not judged as a dressage test and was devised to enable riders to check on their progress and ability.

The paragraph used to open the notes on this test provided by the British Horse Society sums it up as follows:

> To be able to train or improve a horse it is essential that the rider has complete mental and physical control of himself. He must be able to sit in such a position that he is always in balance and harmony with his mount and he must know and be able to use the aids to the degree necessary for each pace and movement.

In his book, *The Foundations of the Classical Art of Riding*, Col Podhajsky says 'I wish once more to sum up those principles which have to be followed in judging a dressage horse and which signify the whole structure of training.

1 A straight horse, moving forward with impulsion.
2 Perfect rhythm and cadence of the different paces—only this rhythm can give real beauty to the dressage horse, producing the same effect as that experienced by listening to good music.
3 A horse must accept the bit quietly and confidently, giving himself willingly and obediently to the guidance of its rider. The horse must look for this guidance from the rider, not the other way round—when the rider uses the reins in order to press the horse into a certain head and neck position. Furthermore, this wrong collection of the horse will always express itself in a lack of freedom in the paces.
4 Alertness achieved by progressive training shows itself in the smoothness of the movements, the fluent transitions and last but not least in absolute balance of the horse in all its paces. This balance can be achieved only if the hindquarters are active enough and take an even part in carry-

ing the weight of the rider. A horse going in such a manner, translated into mechanical terms, will give the impression that the motivating power lies in the hindquarters; this impulsion is guided only by the action of the reins and thus transferred into the right direction. This power must first be created and then controlled by the influence of the reins.

5 The smoothness of the horse which is mainly due to suppleness—complete control of the limbs and perfect balance—will be reflected in the correctness of the various school movements as well as in the sequence of the paces. This smoothness must always be present, not only in the most difficult exercise such as 'Piaffe', 'Passage', 'Pirouette', and 'flying change of legs'—to mention only a few —but also in ordinary collected movements.

6 The obedience of the horse: I purposely mention this chief requirement of a dressage horse last of all, because the obedience is the result of strictly following the other requirements. This obedience must not be that of a circus dog, but the proud result of correct training which has caused the horse to give himself willingly and with pleasure to the indications of the rider.

7

The Hunter

The judging of hunters is a very comprehensive subject as there are such a variety of classes which include the ridden events for model animals up to various weights and, of course, those suitable to carry a lady, as well as the classes for working and small hunters. In addition one includes the breeding and young stock classes, and those at the annual stallion show where the prospective hunter sires are thoroughbreds, most of which have retired from the racecourse.

THE SHOW HUNTER IN RIDDEN EVENTS

Many of the best hunters can be observed in the hunting field rather than the show ring. It is true that some have been ex-show champions but others have never been exhibited. However, the point is what do the judges look for?

Character, courage and sense—a hunter is somehow more a horse than is an elegant lady's hack and he must have the power and ability to cope with a hundred contingencies.

Therefore he needs the strong, properly portioned body and limbs which will carry him through a hard day, the power to gallop on in good or bad going, the heart to cope with an awkward, dangerous or difficult obstacle, and the sense to observe and assess how to tackle his problems without making a fool of himself.

An odd blemish on his limbs or body can be overlooked but never an unsoundness, and of course his wind must be sound. After he has been invited to gallop on, watch your show hunter as he moves parallel with the fence on the far side of the arena—the long side. You will then see if he has that far-reaching, seemingly effortless stride which will carry him a long way. His stride may seem a little short, which means that he must put in the maximum effort to achieve anything like the speed of his free-moving brother, or he may appear to 'go into the ground' instead of over it. Is his action too high off the ground, providing a great display of flailing limbs and feet without covering the distance with the swiftness which is wanted by his rider?

The well-schooled hunter will decrease his speed and pull up in a reasonable time, obediently and without throwing his head about. He must move lightly in fair proportion to his size, not thunder along—of course he cannot help pounding the ground to a certain extent if the going is hard. But at no pace must his action be 'carriagey', resembling that of a carriage horse who carries his head as if he were in harness, bends his knees too much and raises both fore and hind feet just that bit too high, thereby shortening his stride.

He must be well coupled up with no weakness in the back and loins, and his head and neck well set on with a nice length of rein. The latter, or rather the proper juncture of the head and neck, will help him to obey his rider more easily, to give that rider a better ride and to balance himself satisfactorily when he needs to do so.

The different hunter classes are usually divided as follows: those capable of carrying up to 13 stone (lightweight); up to 14½ stone (middleweight); and those able to carry over 14½ stone (heavyweight). If the judges think that an exhibit in the lightweight class is actually up to more weight than 13 stone they can have him transferred then and there to the middleweight event. Sometimes a horse is a borderline case and his owner thinks that his substance and quality will earn him greater success as a lightweight than if he were up against more powerful animals in the middleweight class. Then it is up to the judges to decide where he really belongs.

How does one assess the weight which a horse can carry on a day's hunting? Experience counts here, but a rough indication is the strength and substance of his limbs and back, hock and knee joints, which must be supported by well-shaped, rightly proportioned matching feet. Good strong bone—the cannon bone between the knee and the fetlock joint and its equivalent in the hind legs—is essential but here we must bear in mind the value of the quality of the bone. Quite often a thoroughbred with comparatively light bone will outdo a common horse with bigger bone. He must not be tied in at the knee, nor overtopped with too heavy a body for his legs.

In summing up one can say that it is not always the larger horse which is up to the most weight, but how he is proportioned, plus his good limbs.

The small hunter is confined only by height. He must exceed 14.2hh and not exceed 15.2hh. But like his larger brothers he must be well proportioned, have plenty of quality and show his ability to gallop on.

The lady's hunter must, as we have already said, be suitable to carry a lady. A show hunter's manners should, in any case, pass muster even if such a high degree of co-operation and quiet behaviour as would be expected from a hack is not necessary. Thus the description does not refer specifically to his manners but to the fact that he must be of the right make and shape and move well enough to give his mistress a comfortable ride when he carries a side-saddle.

To achieve this he must have a nice length of rein and a good front, as she does not want to sit right on top of his ears. He must carry his head well, certainly never lean on her hands and his back must be long enough to ensure that the movement of his hindquarters does not jar her as it would if his back was too short. Nor must it be too long and consequently weak. He must be prepared to lead on his off foreleg for his rider, even if she is sitting straight and true in the centre of the saddle, will find this more comfortable although obviously a change of leg is often essential. A smooth, easy ride with a good turn of speed and a willingness to change pace, to steady from the gallop without 'mouthiness' are particularly important in a side-saddle horse. He must be not too narrow of chest, but certainly not too broad, and it is vital that he is a straight mover. True, straight action in a hunter is of the utmost importance and anything else is a weakness, however slight.

In Canada and the United States the hunters are not ridden by the judges but are expected to show a high standard of performance, including jumping.

WORKING HUNTER

In Britain the events for working hunters are very interesting to watch as the markings are as follows: jumping 30; style when jumping 10; conformation 30; ride and presence 30; total obtainable 100. These classes are primarily designed for horses of 15.2hh and over and the rules for judging are compiled by the Hunters Improvement and National Light Horse Breeding Society (see p189).

The minimum number of fences to be negotiated is six and a maximum height of 3ft 9in is allowed at qualifying shows, with 4ft in the final championship competed for at Wembley. It is stated that fences should be of natural appearance and not easily dislodged. The course should not be straightforward but should entail changes of direction. In order to avoid delays and objections the opening and shutting of a gate is not recommended.

Judges are asked to use their discretion as to how to mark the jumping, either each fence individually or the course as a whole. Marks should be deducted for propping into a fence. A fall; hitting a fence hard in front, which might constitute a fall; or refusing should be severely penalised. Style is for a smooth performance and the manner of going of horse and rider at a fair hunting pace.

There is usually a good entry in these events and we often think that if they were graded and handled with imagination they would do much to promote a wide and genuine interest in show classes, encourage newcomers to the ring and even provide a very sensible objective for breeding.

Hunter trials do not perhaps come into the category of show-ring riding as they are carried out over simulated hunting country but here again one may see some first-class performances—as well as some very bad ones. Many of the horses are brilliant, others obviously inexperienced and untrained, and it is important they should be properly schooled before being asked to compete. In the same way many of their riders are gifted and knowledgeable, others do not realise how little they know and this gives their mounts small chance of success.

The British Horse Society issues a simple guide for those interested in hunter trials. In this it states that competitors should go in flights of two, the higher number wearing a sash. In the first round of any class time should only be used to decide the 'time allowed' for the course. The penalties are as follows:

Knocking down an obstacle (other than one classified as fixed)	10 faults
First refusal, circle or runout at an obstacle	10 faults
Second refusal, etc, on the course	10 faults
Third refusal on the course	Elimination
Fall of horse or rider anywhere on the course	30 faults
Jumping wrong panel when in a flight	Elimination
Jumping own panel that has already been knocked down by another competitor	No penalty
Error of course not rectified	Elimination
Exceeding time limit which is twice the time allowed	Elimination

Subject to the nature of the going and the local terrain the 'time allowed' should be based on a speed of 450 yards per minute for all classes except the open, which should use a speed of 500 yards per minute.

HUNTER BREEDING CLASSES

The stallion show held each year by the Hunters Improvement and National Light Horse Breeding Society at the Park Paddocks, Newmarket, has been of considerable help to hunter breeding in Britain. At this show premiums are awarded to those stallions which are considered by the judges as suitable to sire the hunters of the future and whose services would be far too expensive for the pocket of the average breeder. They then travel certain districts and will serve the mares belonging to members of the society at a price within their range.

Super premiums are also awarded and some of the stallions are indeed magnificent. Their pedigrees are most impressive containing famous names such as Big Game, Premonition, Persian Gulf and so on. The 1972 winner at this show of the King George V Champion Challenge Cup was Mr A. C.

Mumford's Quality Fair, who must have established a record as he won this award in 1966 and then again in 1969, 1970 and 1971. He is twelve years old and is by Hook Money, by Bernborough out of Fairy Flower by Fun Fair.

Hunter brood mares, their gay foals and the yearlings, two- and three-year-olds shown in-hand can provide an exhilarating spectacle and plenty of opportunity for heated discussion.

How should one judge a brood mare? Judges have very personal ideas on this and all aspects of judging, but experience is the great and irrefutable answer, particularly in breeding classes. Usually honourably earned scars, blemishes or even unsoundness which will not affect a mare's ability to produce good young stock, are forgiven, but no hereditary disease, unsoundness or weakness.

The judges will expect a brood mare to be generously proportioned and without any defects in her conformation likely to reappear in exaggerated form in her young stock. He will probably look for a noble head, a generous eye, and the loins, limbs and feet which are so vital a part of any worthwhile youngster. He will also note whether she herself is so made that her movement is automatically free and her stride sufficiently lengthy, that there is width across her hips and that her back is sufficiently—not exaggeratedly—long, with well-sprung ribs. For good measure, add depth of girth and plenty of bone.

It is usually agreed that the judging of foals is a tricky business. As regards size much depends on the foaling date— some of those you see in the ring may have been foaled much earlier than others, had the right attention and a better chance to mature. Gay, gangling little objects perhaps, but even their apparent lack of proportion is not necessarily deceptive if you look for good limbs plus a certain amount of proportion, strong little loins and a nice head.

Proportion, development and the general points of a good

horse, together with free forward movement must all be watched for in the various in-hand age groups. Sometimes a two-year-old is so nice an animal he will beat a three-year-old, equally the more developed youngster may well defeat his younger brother or sister. If fillies are judged with colts or with geldings this is a pity as it may lead to trouble and in any case makes the class uneven. A filly must have feminine characteristics and a colt or gelding must be masculine. In young stock this is more pronounced than in ridden classes where the animals are more mature and schooled to carry out a certain job.

It is amusing to watch these classes and to imagine how these youngsters will develop and whether they will make a career for themselves in some special walk of equine life. Have we seen a future champion hack, a hunter, a show-jumper, a winner at Badminton Horse Trials, or just a beloved and clever-footed companion?

Page 111 A Spotted Horse with leopard markings, Shanghai, owned by Miss Susan Barker. He has won many competitions

Page 112 (*above*) A typical Connemara brood mare, Miss P. Lyne's champion Arctic Moon. Both strongly made and graceful, she carries herself well and is ready for any kind of job. Note her light dun colour and black points; (*below*) Mirth, a beautifully produced and perfectly made pony, suitable for the smaller child, and with the ideal pony head which is important

Page 113 (*above*) This Appaloosa stallion is owned by Col V. D. S. Williams.
The forepart of his body is mottled, the loins and hip white and his nostrils
and lips are parti-coloured; (*below*) Mrs E. Thomas's Palomino mare Kingsettle Pagoda. She won the Palomino championship and the supreme in-hand
championship at Yateley against strong competition

Page 114 Mr Gregory Lougher, a great American horseman and a judge at America's largest Western show at the Cow Palace, San Francisco. He is riding his young Quarter Horse stallion, Clover Drift, in a hackamore with heavy rope reins, as used in the first stages of training

8

Our Beautiful Ponies

Some of the most valuable and well-loved of all equine breeds
are the ponies—children's show ponies, mountain and moorland ponies and those expensive and beautiful creatures which
have evolved as a result of wise crossing. The history of their
parents and grandparents on both sides of the family would
often be quite a remarkable saga.

SHOW PONIES

These include the ponies in the ridden classes for those of
12.2hh and under, 13.2hh and under, and 14.2hh and under.
Certain wise rules for judging, issued by the British Show
Pony Society at the time of writing, are as follows:

1   No person may deliberately enter and show a pony
under a judge who is known to have bred, sold, or produced that pony.

G

2   Once a judge has commenced judging a class a pony may not be led or ridden out of the ring without the permission of the judge.

3   Once a class has started there shall be no change of rider. This does not include a change of rider from showing class to championship class, if this were found necessary.

4   All judges must take a pony's manners into consideration when judging.

5   12.2hh ponies must not be galloped in their classes. If the judge, or judges, however, are unable to reach a decision regarding the first three ponies they are permitted to gallop them, but not more than one at a time. (Incidentally we will here confirm that the ponies are allowed to canter quietly round in their event, although they are very wisely barred from galloping as they may upset one another, get out of control through excitement and so on, if encouraged to tear round the ring in large numbers.) No cantering is allowed in the first ridden pony class, except for individual performances.

6   13.2hh and 14.2hh ponies may be galloped in their classes at the judge's discretion, but not more than four at a time.

7   Championships—if it is necessary to gallop 12.2hh ponies, it is a condition that they are galloped singly and not at the same time as 13.2hh and 14.2hh ponies.

8   If in the opinion of the judges a pony is considered to be unsound, the exhibitor should be given the option of withdrawing the exhibit from the class or asking that the official veterinary surgeon should examine the pony. The veterinary surgeon's decision is final.

9   The wearing of spurs in junior ridden show pony classes is forbidden.

10   All three-year-old ponies must be shown in snaffle

bridles as well as those in novice classes or leading rein or first ridden pony classes.

11 Any pony may be exhibited in a plain snaffle bridle if considered suitable by the owner. This is plain, straight or jointed in the middle.

12 Ponies can be unshod at the discretion of their owners.

13 Ponies shown in the following classes must be four years old or over: leading rein, first ridden pony, pairs, side-saddle, open classes, novice classes held up till and including the end of June of the year in question, open pony championship classes.

14 Three-year-old ponies must be shown in novice classes only on or after July 1st of the year in question, held at affiliated shows. They must be shown in snaffle bridles only and will not be allowed to compete in open championship classes. They will be allowed to be treated as novices for the season 1 July until 31 December and will still be novice at the beginning of their season as a four-year-old.

15 All ridden show pony classes must be restricted to mares and geldings only. Mares with living foals born during the current season will not be shown in saddle classes.

It may seem that there are a great many rules which exhibitors need to observe but owing to the existing interest in showing ponies which seems to have become almost a part of our national life, it has been necessary to make these rules. They are the result of practical experience and are designed to help rather than hinder. They are essential as a framework for the benefit and welfare of the ponies, their riders and their owners. It is, of course, possible that the wise and active committee of the British Show Pony Society may have occasion to change them to suit the circumstance of the moment, but details and confirmation can always be obtained from the secretary (see p188).

In the leading rein classes the judge looks for a pony with sufficient substance to give confidence to his small and inexperienced rider, a head and neck carried at a comfortable and reassuring angle, an easy-to-ride action in walk and trot, and an equitable temperament, plus the usual points of a well-made pony.

It should never be flashy, too wide or too narrow, and must be shown in a snaffle bit. Riders of these animals must not compete in other show pony classes. The expert, knowledgeable child rider showing off a leading rein pony is an anomaly, for this type of pony and of class is intended expressly for the very young beginner.

Something more is expected of the 12.2hh show pony. Not only must he be a model of his kind, a perfect miniature pony, but he must have a nice length of stride which will enable his rider to take part efficiently in Pony Club events, go hunting and so on. He must carry his small, clever head well, move freely and obediently and understand the aids sufficiently to give a nice little individual show. Above all he must have good manners. He must be neither weedy nor over-solid but have a sufficiency of quality to hold his own in any company—this does not mean that he needs to look like a small thoroughbred.

It is important that that elusive quality 'pony character' is seen in all show ponies but this may sometimes be less obvious in the 14.2hh and 13.2hh classes, especially the former. Often larger animals tend towards the hunter or hack types and cease to be true ponies, although too small for these other classes. Many a judge has had to make a difficult decision when choosing between what amounts to a very good small hunter and a true pony which lacks perhaps the quality or the movement, or the schooling of his fellow competitor. Thus some, but not many shows, hold classes for children's hunter ponies and there are now an increasing number of events for the working hunter pony, which are classified by the British Show Pony Society. These classes vary from the nursery stakes for ponies not over 13hh to stiffer events for those not exceeding 15hh. The rules, riders' age limits, fences, jumping penalties and marking are all clearly defined by this society. These events should provide plenty of scope for the good, useful pony of all sizes and description.

We see very lovely ponies in the 13.2hh model show classes, elegant, well-schooled, carrying themselves and their riders with grace and pride. Many are descended from other retired show ponies which have been crossed with good pony stallions, Arabs or thoroughbreds. They often carry a substantial percentage of the invaluable mountain and moorland pony blood. Their breeding is not however the subject of this book but how the end product is judged.

How would you judge them and what would you watch for? Imagine that you are in the centre of the ring and list the things you would do and why, then compare your notes with the following few suggestions, bearing in mind that a fair standard of performance and manners are essential in the 13.2hh class and an even higher, slightly more advanced one in the 14.2hh as ponies in this event are intended for older and presumably more advanced, ambitious riders. Their training should be sufficient to enable them to be very useful in any sphere of pony life, and many are worth a great deal of money.

When you watch them circle the ring you will see if they are free movers, ridden on a comfortable rein, carrying their heads proudly and not throwing them about or fighting their bits. A good pony has the self-confidence, the pride and the presence of a hack, gay when he is young, yet still never losing his regal air when he is old and has lost just a little of his breathtaking grace and freedom of action.

You will also take note of their general make and shape, which you will be able to assess better when they have been lined up and their saddles are off—occasionally a pony will disappoint very much when he is stripped. He may have a mean back, his withers and shoulders show to great disadvantage or his depth of girth or general proportions look less useful than when he was being cleverly shown to advantage by his rider.

As you inspect each one you will note his head, eyes, neat little ears, the way his neck joins his head and enables him to bridle without difficulty, and how it joins his shoulders in a nice sweep. Are his shoulders well laid back? Has he a strong forearm, a nice length of bone? Is he tied in at the knees (it is better that he should be over at the knees than tied in directly underneath this joint), are his fetlocks in good trim or have they become rounded with work, are there signs of splints, or side bones or even ringbone? Has he good matching, open feet, strong hocks, strong loins, his tail well set on? These are the type of things that you should look for.

Make sure when he is run up in-hand by his rider that his action is true and straight in front, no plaiting etc, and this also applies behind—you must note that he does not go too wide as this is a sign of weakness. But on this point be a little merciful in the case of a young pony.

We think each judge has his or her own particular slight preference as, for example, good movement. One is prepared to forgive certain small sins to a good mover with a long elastic stride. In judging ponies in a championship there is so much in the balance because not many can boast an equal proportion of beauty, quality, manners, pony type, perfect limbs, conformation and movement! Those who have it all are worth, and indeed fetch, a fortune. One can assume that if the pony has reached the championship he has not much wrong with him and it is therefore up to you to choose the most perfect specimen, irrespective of size. But what about age?

On this question there can be no final ruling because the youngster must eventually replace the older pony if showing is to be of any value, yet if the old pony is still at his zenith in spite of his age and is just that bit better and more experienced he has every right to hold his own. But not if he is beginning to go down hill. As we have said elsewhere, the wise owner will retire his champion from the ring and let him lead a more ordinary life before this moment occurs.

We would like to finish this section with an extract from an article by Davina Whiteman, which appeared in *Riding*. She has trained, exhibited and gained supreme championships with an impressive number of ponies.

The primary task of any trainer is to maintain the natural balance, rhythm and presence of the pony, whilst teaching and conditioning him to carry the extra burden of a rider. I add presence to balance and rhythm, because I feel that often during breaking or training the spirit of the animal is broken either by lack of food, or by forcing him to do something beyond his capacity. In either case the animal loses his zest for living and his willingness to please his master.

These words of Mrs Whiteman's should help you to realise and to evaluate the behaviour of the good show pony and to appreciate the shortsightedness of not giving him fair and sensible treatment.

WORKING HUNTER PONIES

These classes vary from the nursery stakes over low fences for ponies not over 13hh to stiffer events for those not exceeding 15hh and should provide plenty of scope for the good, useful pony of all sizes and descriptions. Riders' age limits and further details are available from the British Show Pony Society.

The classes are judged in two phases. In phase one they are expected to jump a minimum of five fences, the height depending on the class and, of course, the size of the pony. These fences must be of hunting type, built with rustic material and as substantial as possible and must include a spread. The course must include a change of direction.

This phase is carried out first and any pony which is eliminated is not required for the final judging. The British Show Pony Society suggests that if possible two judges should be appointed, one to judge the jumping phase, the other to judge phase two immediately phase one has been completed. Both judges will come together for the final judging.

In phase two the ponies must walk, trot, canter and gallop. A hunter type pony is looked for, one with quality that will carry a child across country when following hounds.

It is essential that the judge of the jumping phase should have an assistant who will be a competent marker, and that the official marking sheets of the British Show Pony Society are used.

Jumping penalties are as follows:

First refusal	10
Second refusal	20
Third refusal	Elimination
Knock down	10
Fall of horse or rider	20

A complete turn round constitutes a refusal

Marking:

Phase one, jumping	50
Style and manners	10
Phase two, conformation, freedom of action, manners	40
	———
	100

BREEDING CLASSES

The classes for young stock, and for brood mares, as well as for pony stallions must be judged with a happy adjustment of concentration and experience. In the last-named class the judge must remember that the stallion's good or bad characteristics will be carried forward in successive generations and that he must be of the type to breed a good pony. Sometimes a less brilliant but uniform and well-proportioned animal is the answer but so much depends on so many things it is impossible to judge this class on paper or by rule of thumb.

The brood mares need the same points as hunter brood mares—quality, substance and a certain roominess, providing, of course, that they are of good pony type.

There is often strong competition and certainly variety in the young stock classes. Here again one can only choose the best of its type, providing all the essentials are there (good feet, limbs and general proportions), bearing in mind that growth and in some cases the gangliness of youth can mislead. Not always the youngster which is apparently the best on the day is the best at maturity.

MOUNTAIN AND MOORLAND PONIES

Up to a point the main principles of judging apply equally to each mountain and moorland breed, but no judge who is not conversant with the main features of the breed in question should judge it, as the winner must be true to type. For example, the action of the Fell pony is not the same or expected to be the same as that of a Connemara. Each breed was at some time used for a specific purpose and its inbred characteristics are invaluable for cross-breeding providing that the breed itself has been kept pure.

Dartmoor. This is a lovely riding pony, originally able to carry men on the moor when they were looking for their farm stock.

123

The stallions must have very strong backs and limbs, powerful necks, fine heads beautifully shaped, small, pointed ears and good feet to help them to traverse successfully the bogs, the tors, the clitters. Their manes and tails are magnificent and their height must not exceed 12.2hh. There is no colour bar, except piebalds and skewbalds, but excessive white is not encouraged. The mares are generously made and the mature pony which is shown either in-hand or under saddle is an attractive little animal of considerable scope and intelligence —they are naturally good jumpers.

Exmoor. This pony is immensely hardy and strong, and makes excellent foundation stock. They should never be weakly in appearance. The height limit is 12.2hh for mares and 12.3hh for stallions. The colours bay, dun or brown are accepted, but never white hairs or white markings anywhere, and the muzzle is always mealy, ie a shade of oatmeal. The pure-bred Exmoor has a wide forehead with prominent and beautiful eyes, sometimes called 'toad-eyes' because the lids are slightly hooded; short, thick pointed ears, of a mealy colour inside, and nicely flaring nostrils. The coat is a useful protection against the extremes of winter on Exmoor, harsh and springy, carrying no bloom in winter, but close, hard and shining in the summer. Foals have a thick woolly undercoat and the top coat comprises long, harsh hairs which direct the rain downwards so that it cannot penetrate.

Connemara. These ponies usually vary from 13 to 14hh although no precise measurement is issued by the British Connemara Society and their accepted colours are bay, black, grey, brown and dun, also chestnut and roan, though these are less common. Many of the best have been grey. They should have a certain individuality of appearance, should be graceful and most certainly strong, never weeds. The stallions should have good loins and limbs and this pony, though not big, should be so proportioned as to be able to carry a fair amount of weight

—not too long in the back, deep enough in the body, with nice sloping shoulders.

Dale. We do not see many of these ponies at the shows although they have quite a following in the north and many are owned by miners. Look always for a hardy, very strong pony whose height must not exceed 14.2hh, bearing in mind that he must be able to work on the hilly, northern farms. This is where his stamina stands him in good stead as he will carry a shepherd over large areas of the dales as well as carry out the farm work to which a bigger horse would be unsuited. He must have a short back with strong loins, quarters and thighs, hard, well-shaped feet and true showy action at the trot. Fine, silky hair is allowed on the heels. They are mostly black in colour but bays, browns and occasionally greys are found.

Fell. This pony bears a resemblance to his Dales brother, but he is more of a riding pony—both a powerful and a graceful one. The height limit is 14hh but they usually average from 13hh to 14hh. The colour is preferably black, brown, grey or bay with no white markings, although a star or a little white on the feet is permissible. Their heads are small and well chiselled and their manes and tails very beautiful, with fine hair (not coarse) at the heels. Their action at the walk should be smart and true, the trot well-balanced all round with good knee and hock action, and they should be able to show great pace and endurance, bringing the hind legs well under the body when going.

Highland. The true Highland pony must have no white marks although the eel and dorsal stripe along his back and the zebra markings on the leg are correct. It is believed that yellow dun was the original colour—the real yellow dun looks smoky black at the roots of the hair, changing to golden towards the tips. But more often you will see this immensely powerful and so beautiful pony in shades of grey and cream, or chestnut with a silver mane and tail, or blue, silver and mouse dun.

There are two types, the smaller pure-bred from 13 to 14hh, the larger Highland Garron is 14 to 14.2hh. The smaller Highland pony has a beautiful head, wide between the eyes, and very neat little prick ears.

Their legs must be strong and of a length proportionate to their height, with closely placed hocks, sloping pasterns (not too long) and round, open feet. The only hair on their legs consists of small silken tufts on the fetlocks, and their luxuriant manes and tails must be silky to the touch, not harsh or wiry. Neither the larger nor smaller ponies should have disproportionately large heads, hairy noses or too much hair on the heels or coronet. They are expected to move freely and well.

New Forest pony. There are two types of New Forest pony. Although the overall height limit is 14.2hh, the first is up to 13.2hh and is lighter than the larger one which is up to 14.2hh with plenty of bone and substance. Either are very useful ponies and equally popular. The average height is about 13.1hh. They can be of any colour except piebald or skewbald. The head is well set on and although the neck is a little short from throat to chest, the good, well laid-back shoulder gives a sufficient length of rein. The back is short, loins and quarters good with the tail well set on but not exaggeratedly high.

Shetland. This pony is remarkable for his strength and also for his intelligence and independence in relation to his size which must not exceed 40in in height at three years old and 42in at four years old and over. To watch these ponies proceeding with determination—and sometimes saying what they think about it—at one of the Ponies of Britain Shows is enough to give any judge a headache. Which offers the best overall picture? It should comprise a shapely head, broad between the eyes, a neck with sufficient crest, rising strongly from a well-laid, oblique shoulder, a body with a broad chest, short back and strong quarters, with muscular loins, an abundant mane and tail, the latter set fairly high.

His forelegs must be well-placed under the shoulder, with a well-muscled forearm, strong knees, good bone and springy pasterns. Much the same description applies to the hind legs, not forgetting that the thighs should be strong and muscular, the feet open, round and tough and the action true, with each joint fully used. The Shetland is indeed a bundle of strength but he must never look clumsy or ill-proportioned. There is no colour bar.

Welsh. To those unacquainted with the judging of the Welsh pony there are five sections in the Welsh Stud Book, as follows: Section A is devoted to the Welsh Mountain pony which must not exceed 12hh. Section B is for the riding pony not over 13.2hh. Section C is for the pony of cob type, not over 13.2hh, and Section D for cobs over this height. Section E is for geldings which are the progeny of a Foundation Stock 1 mare and a fully registered stallion. FS1 means that one parent is registered.

The description Foundation Stock or FS is a little confusing. Briefly it indicates that FS are approved ponies. In the case of FS1, one parent is registered (if filly, FS2; a colt if gelded becomes Section E which is for geldings only). An FS mare may be put to a fully registered stallion and her filly is then FS2, her colt will be gelded and becomes Section E. If an FS2 is put to a fully registered stallion and produces a filly, the filly can then be fully registered as an approved pony, ie Foundation Stock.

Remember when watching a class for Welsh Mountain ponies that they must be graceful, strong and well proportioned, with those perfect hindquarters which cannot be described as cobby, goose-rumped or ragged—certainly never weak, or with a low-set tail. The jaws and throat of his neat and charming little head must be cleanly cut with plenty of room at the angle of jaw, thus enabling him to carry it well and to bridle as he should. He too has a luxuriant mane and tail and any colour is allowed except piebald or skewbald. Watch him move and make sure that the action is true, graceful, straight and almost effortless.

The stallion should move with great dash, his strides eating up the ground, not just displaying undue action and making little progress; the mare does not emulate the stallion but moves freely with strides proportionate to her size. The young stock are gay, free, straight movers, not too wide or too narrow in front or behind.

The Welsh riding pony Section B is showy and very beautiful. Thanks to his breeding, the background provided by his forefathers and his excellent make and shape he will be capable of all kinds of work, such as hunting, cross-country riding, etc. Sometimes these ponies are bred carelessly and are weaklings, and this should be guarded against. The object is to market them quickly, as there is such a demand; but the good Welsh Section B is quite a different proposition and a pony which is well worth owning.

Remember all these things when making your choice of the best pony in the class in which you are interested, whether it is a ridden or an in-hand breeding class. Naturally the ridden and the in-hand events cannot be judged in the same fashion. For example, stallions must be considered with a view to the qualities and characteristics they are likely to hand on, not necessarily and only on their suitability, appearance and performance in a ridden event.

The Welsh cobs have been dealt with in Chapter 4.

The geldings, Section E, are judged simply as ponies, but they usually compete in other events, not just in classes confined to Section E exhibits only. This section is intended chiefly for purposes of registration.

9

Fairy-tale Horses: the Palomino, the Appaloosa and the Spotted

THE PALOMINO

Perhaps one of the most romantic and glamorous of all our horses and ponies is the Palomino, who should be richly golden, with a pure white mane and tail. If he is of the right make and shape, moves regally and is also of the correct colour he is of breathtaking loveliness, but, alas, it is not easy to combine together all these fine qualities in one equine form. In fact, the unfortunate judge, having watched them all circle the ring and chosen what *may* be the best animal, may find himself disillusioned when all are lined up and he is examining them for possible defects, or shall we say weaknesses. He may have a challenging job in weighing up conflicting points.

The classes are not easy to judge as the Palomino is a colour and not a breed. Not only may there be an assortment of good and indifferent animals from which to choose, but there are also problems connected with the colour of body, eyes, tail etc. Not many Palominos retain their colour perfectly throughout the years, and some always change to a certain extent when they grow their new coats in the spring and autumn. But a few do remain gloriously golden all their lives, with snow-white manes and tails which are never flaxen or silver.

One must always watch for any definite leaning towards chestnut in their colour scheme—this is a major fault. So is a tendency towards dirty cream, or towards a darkness which can so easily become 'a coat of another colour'; it is better for a young Palomino to be too light than too dark because as he grows to maturity his coat will almost certainly darken and if it is too dark already it is unlikely that it will turn to gold.

The correct shade at maturity should be the colour of a newly minted sovereign and no more than three shades lighter or darker are accepted for registration. White markings are not allowed anywhere on the body, only on the face and legs. The mane and tail must always be inspected with care as no more than 15 per cent chestnut or dark hairs are allowed to sully their purity. Eyes must be dark brown, with a hazel or black iris and both of the same colour—no wall eyes allowed. Under the rules of the British Palomino Society the skin colour must be dark.

The judging of colour in the young stock classes, although meticulous is not quite as rigorous as in the adult. The latter is accepted for permanent registration at six years of age or over, by which time it is hoped and believed that his colour will have been confirmed and that it is now definite except for some slight modification at the change of the seasons. Naturally at any age good, uniform colour, conformation and action will always take precedence over those animals who fail in any one

Page 131 (*above*) Mr Lougher riding his Quarter Horse mare, Clover Lori, which he bred. Having passed the primary hackamore stage, she now wears a single curb bit with a lightweight bosal; (*below*) Mrs Anne Hyland, a member of the Western Horsemen's Association of Great Britain, riding her Western Pleasure Horse, Jacobite, imported from the USA

Page 132 (*above*) Bill Steinkraus, captain of the American show-jumping team, riding Sinjan at Hickstead. His team won the silver medal at the 1972 Olympic Games at Munich; (*below*) Tommy Brennan, negotiating the bank on Donegal, when competing in the British Jumping Derby at Hickstead

Page 133 David Broome, who has the gift of making most horses go well for him. He will always be remembered for his handling of Sunsalve, who was indeed a difficult ride but a brilliant performer in David's capable hands. Here he is riding Nathan

Page 134 (*above*) Douglas Bunn, who brought into being the famous show-jumping centre at his home at Hickstead, near Brighton in Sussex, riding Beethoven; (*below*) Alan Oliver riding John Glenn

of these respects.

The colour is said to be of Arab origin in the far distant past and indeed classes for registered part-bred Arab Palominos have been held regularly at the Arab show. As well as Palomino horses there are many good Palomino ponies, quite a few of which are Welsh. The National Palomino Championship features a class for fully registered Welsh ponies, Sections A, B, C or D.

The Palomino is of world-wide popularity—in America, Australia, Spain and many other countries. Indeed, Spain is seldom prepared to allow her best stock to go for export.

But the question of how to breed a good Palomino is not easy to answer as the colour does not breed true. The crosses most likely to bring worthwhile results are between Palomino and Palomino or Palomino and chestnut, from either of which there is a 50 per cent chance of a Palomino-coloured foal. Other crosses may also prove successful but the anticipated ratio of Palomino foals may be less.

Any further information about these very showy animals, the classes which are held at various shows throughout the season and their own annual championship fixture is available from the British Palomino Society (see p188).

THE APPALOOSA

This is an extremely ancient breed which nearly died out in America—it did at one time become extinct until imported by the invading Spanish conquistadores during the sixteenth century. Later it might again have met with the same fate but for the Nez Perce Indians who bred, wisely and with discrimination, great herds of them.

This horse had the requisite stamina, size and temperament, in addition to its unusual colouring, and was used to hunt bear, elk and buffalo and to carry braves in time of battle. Now they

135

H

are needed largely as cow ponies and pleasure horses, as well as for trial riding, polo and show-jumping.

One must remember that all Appaloosas are not spotted, just as all Spotted Horses are not Appaloosas. Some Appaloosas are whole-coloured, the mares being mottled roan over the entire body. Their colouring is unusual, as nostrils and lips are parti-coloured and the sclera of the eyes is white. Sometimes the forepart of the body is one colour, sometimes a mottled roan, and the loins and hips are lighter in colour, or else white with dark, round or egg-shaped spots. Other Appaloosas are white, covered with leopard spot markings. Their feet, of which the horn is very dense, frequently have vertical black and white stripes.

The Appaloosa varies in height from 14.2hh to 15hh. He is a compact and most useful horse with powerful quarters and he should be judged on his own qualities and make and shape, not as a thoroughbred. This is always an important axiom of judging; judge a breed or class on its own merits, on what it is supposed to be and to do, not on pre-conceived notions or a rigid rule, other than that laid down in the schedule of the show, of course.

THE SPOTTED

The Spotted Horse or Pony may result from very mixed breeding, either good or bad, so you must judge on two things: his merit as an animal and his colouring. This can give rise to quite a lot of anxious thought. Let us suppose that a well-made horse who is also a good mover is not quite as admirably or correctly marked as his humbler brother, whose make, shape and quality leave a little to be desired. Which should head the line?

It is not possible to give an absolutely direct answer to this question when it refers to imaginary animals. One must *see* them—see how they move, note their potentialities and really assess the difference in the markings. Willy nilly, and without weakness or a leaning either way it is sometimes necessary to decide (or err, if you wish) in one way, sometimes another, depending on how much or how little there is to choose between them. I admit that one must never forget with any coloured horse (and in this I include Palominos) that colour is of the utmost importance, remembering at the same time that a badly made animal is a disgrace to his colour or breed.

However, to cheer prospective judges let me add here that the society devoted to the Spotted Horse and Pony (see p189) tries to ensure that no really indifferent animal is accepted for registration or is eligible to compete. This society wishes to improve the breed and, indeed, establish it.

Spotted Horses as well as Appaloosas have been known for centuries, and certain breeds in Europe, for instance the old Danish breed of Knabstruppers, consist entirely of 'Spotteds'.

The marks are as follows:

Leopard spots of any colour on a white or light-coloured background.

Blanket, a white rump or back on whicn there are spots of any colour.

Snowflake, white spots on a foundation of any colour.

Piebalds, skewbalds and dapple greys are not eligible.

Typical characteristics consist of white sclera round the eye, similar to the white round a human eye, also striped hooves of yellowish white and black or brown in vertical stripes. The bare skin is mottled, usually under the dock, on the udder and round the eyes and muzzle. Manes and tails are often very sparse.

10

Western Horsemanship Classes

Interest in Western horsemanship began when a senior captain with BOAC, who had ridden Western in Canada, Brazil and Chile and found it much to his liking, decided to retire to Burley, in the New Forest; such was his enthusiasm that he and his wife opened the Flying G Ranch in 1961 to cater for holidaymakers and the very few who were then proficient in the Western way of riding. Other enthusiasts followed suit and there are now several flourishing and fully-booked ranches in the south of England, with others planned for the South East.

The first ever Western Pleasure Horse class took place in the late sixties, when over thirty riders turned up from all parts of the country; some of the tack was weird and wonderful, as was most of the riding, but the enthusiasm was there too and soon afterwards the Western Horseman's Association of Great Britain was born (see p189). Thanks to the efforts of the late

Mrs Kay Moseley it became affiliated to the British Horse Society in 1969 and with this official recognition and raised status now has members all over the country and abroad. The membership at the time of writing is about 600. The president is Lt-Col R. B. Moseley, and in 1971 the Western Horseman's Association established a Registry of Quarter-horses in Great Britain, the late Kay Moseley's Hollywood Cotton being the foundation stallion.

The association produces an excellent newsletter each month. It not only contains up-to-date, detailed information, but also has comments from members. The association is still trying to disassociate itself from the popular conception of Western riding as English cowboys in fancy dress galloping about hooting and hollering and armed to the teeth with fake guns, but it is making slow progress. There have been most unfortunate TV films and newspaper publicity stressing this aspect of so-called 'riding', those taking part in the various stunts having no connection whatsoever with the Western Horseman's Association.

Basic training of the Western Pleasure Horse is of course similar to the basic training of any horse, the same applying to the rider, the object being to produce an animal which is a pleasure to ride. It is interesting to note how quickly a horse well-schooled under English saddle will adapt to Western saddle; a case in point is the Arab stallion Rabalain, imported from California, who headed the ridden stallion class at the 1971 Royal International Horse Show. Ridden by Mrs Chris Massey, he goes equally well under any saddle, including side-saddle, as does another American import, Mrs Ann Hyland's Jacobite and the Fairfield Arabian Stud's stallion, Hassani.

Rabalain has also had a number of other successes in the show ring, including a second prize in the class for ridden Arabs at the Royal International Horse Show in 1972, and several firsts, also one championship and one reserve championship at the Arab show, as well as two firsts at the Hampshire Horse Show.

Dandi, owned and ridden by another member, Gary Davies, has accomplished two 1,000-mile treks, as Golden Horseshoe qualifiers and in the 1972 Golden Horseshoe ride, where they received a silver medal, and is always in tip-top condition. Gary prefers to ride under Western saddle and did so in the Golden Horseshoe qualifier in 1971. Both Gary and Dandi are extremely modest and are deserving of far more public recognition, particularly as Gary is a comparatively novice rider; what he has been able to accomplish should also be possible for other riders with non-show horses who are willing to take the trouble to join in this new type of adventure. They should also be an object lesson to the many more experienced riders whose animals failed to pass the veterinary checks at the Golden Horseshoe Ride in the autumn of 1972.

For non-competitors there is an annual round-up or Western weekend where members and enthusiasts from all over the country get together, and weekends in various parts of the country with their traditional barbecues and square-dancing. Those who now ride Western for pleasure, as opposed to their normal hunting and show-jumping activities, find it a more relaxed form of equitation; a few with back problems have found it the answer and most enjoy the lack of formality, rules and regulations regarding dress, each item of which has a purpose.

Spectators at Western Pleasure Horse classes which are held at a number of different shows, will note that judges penalise extreme speed; the paces required being the uncollected walk, the jog and the lope or canter, and neck-reining is obligatory. Performance receives 60 per cent of the marks, neatness of horse and rider 25 per cent, and conformation 15 per cent, and only humane-type Western bits are allowed.

The correct dress (jeans, plain or check shirts, Western

boots and hat) is neat and functional, and plain working saddles are preferred; any abuse of the optional spurs is heavily penalised. In showing classes there is little formality, the ideal being correct but not showy dress and a well-mannered and well-turned out horse or pony which understands the aids given by the rider.

The Western Horseman's Association is most anxious to avoid any anglicising of these Western classes, thus producing a hybrid which bears no relation to either style, and therefore encourages demonstrations and displays by experts so that the public can see a properly trained horse and rider. On the lighter side, there are trail classes, similar to the English handy pony, in which horse and rider cope with various obstacles; barrel-racing, and even a mounted Western square-dancing team which has been popular at several shows.

The tack used in the Western Pleasure Horse class consists of any Western-type saddle with saddle blanket; any Western bridle or hackamore; any humane-type Western bit; no chain or rawhide under the jaws, curb straps to be of leather, at least $\frac{1}{2}$in wide; split reins are mandatory unless hackamore, roping or California-style reins with romal are used; no martingale or tie-down, and a breast-collar is optional.

The same rules regarding tack apply to a trail class, except that a lariat or slicker or raincoat must be carried. A canteen is optional but if a bosal or California closed reins are used, hobbles will be carried. Horses must walk, jog and lope and negotiate six to eight obstacles—some of these are not so much obstacles as tests of handiness or obedience, ie dragging a log or bale backwards and forwards or using rope round the saddlehorn.

It is permissible to change the reining hand when carrying out this part of the trail class but in the Western Pleasure Horse class reins must be held in one hand only, with no changing of hands during the class. Markings in the trail class

141

are: performance 75 per cent, condition and neatness of horse and rider 25 per cent.

In the Western Stock class, the dress and tack are as for Western Pleasure. A lariat must be carried, also hobbles if closed reins are used. Competitors will enter the ring as a group and after jogging and loping at the judge's request will line up or retire from ring at the judge's discretion whilst each competitor works individually at:

1 Quick start and sliding stop.
2 Settle horse, 10 seconds and back up.
3 Small figure of eight slowly.
4 Large figure of eight, fast.
5 Ground tie (or hobble, if closed reins are used).
6 Rope test.

In this class overall smoothness will be looked for as well as a horse which is both obedient to the bit and working off the haunches; failure to change front and hind leads in the figure eights will be penalised; holding any part of the saddle automatically disqualifies. Marking in stock classes are: performance 75 per cent, conformation 15 per cent, turnout 10 per cent.

There are many other classes, including very simple ones for novices, but those which we have described will give you an idea of how they are judged and what the exhibitors are expected to do. They certainly differ in many respects from the usual show-ring events.

11

Jumpers and Jumping: Explanations and Comments

The remarkable understanding, respect and trust which can and does exist between certain horses and riders in the various competitive events, particularly show-jumping, is not always fully realised by the spectator. Some horses are nervous or excitable and with an uneducated rider or someone who is not just on their wavelength they will make quite spectacular mistakes, yet achieve brilliant success in the right hands. Others are placid, their only need a little encouragement, or are great-hearted; or stupid; or more than a little intelligent and well aware what it is all about. Each has to learn by experience.

There are a number of recorded cases of horses which have never been looked upon as potential jumpers but have in fact fallen into the hands of an average but not brilliant horseman,

143

who with equestrian tact, courage and determination have got them going right—have gained their confidence—and they eventually have won show-jumping competitions.

Unorthodox horsemanship is harmless, it usually stems from some good reason, but bad riding is a disaster. It may come from impatience, unwillingness to learn, lack of self-discipline or bad instruction. The first and absolute essential is a good strong seat in the saddle—why so many people side-step the importance of achieving this is something hard to understand. Until it has been acquired the instructor, no matter how good or how advanced, can do nothing for his pupil.

Let us first look at a course which has been laid out for a good jumping competition. Each obstacle has its hazards and the approach, the leap, the landing and the move onward towards the next jump require not only thought but knowledge and an ability to adjust in a flash. This in turn means mental and physical fitness as well as suppleness in the rider, whereas the horse must be bold, obedient and free, observant and able to bend in any direction. Add to it the side-effects of the horse's temperament and that of his rider. One slight maladjustment will throw the whole machine out of balance and cause an irreparable mistake. It takes a lot of work, astuteness and dedication to produce the good show-jumper, whether two or four-legged.

Possibly you have noticed that some horses are particularly suited to competitions which are 'against the clock'. Others are better fitted to jump a big course in which time is not as vital but in which the heights and types of the fences might well prove too much for the speed merchants.

The following passage describes how the horse jumps. It comes from the official manual of the United States Cavalry School, edited for civilian riders by Gordon Wright and entitled *The Cavalry Manual of Horsemanship and Horsemastership* (1962).

An animal with a short neck, such as a deer or dog, when jumping a high fence, pops almost straight up into the air, and lands on all fours simultaneously. A horse, on the contrary, by using his head and neck as a balancer, describes a graceful parabola, with his forefeet coming to the ground well in advance of the hind. *It is an interesting fact that the forefeet strike the ground and leave it again before the hind feet touch.* Inasmuch as this see-saw, or bascule movement is accomplished as a result of the employment of the head and neck, the necessity for the rider's not interfering with the movements of the head and neck during a jump, is evident. All have seen a poor rider hanging onto the reins and pulling the horse's head high in the air, over the top of a jump. With his neck thus immobilised, the poor horse also lands on all fours simultaneously, and is said to 'jump like a deer'.

In approaching an obstacle, a horse that jumps in good form, lowers and extends his neck in an easy, graceful position, in order to estimate the character and height of the obstacle, as well as his point of take-off. Very often he may be seen extending his neck and head far to the front with a very swift gesture, just before his front feet leave the ground. This gesture apparently is made for the purpose of producing a counteracting force to the rear, permitting him to check and shorten his last strides in placing himself for his take-off. Also with an extended neck, he can exert its greatest force in its next and most important gesture. *Thus, during the approach, the rider's hands should be passive and exceedingly elastic, softly following all the forward and backward movements of the horse's head.*

The exceedingly graceful and most effective style of the American show-jumping riders, both men and women, whom we have watched in Britain and on the Continent, no doubt results from the simple but essential principles which are now laid down in this book, perfected by the teaching of their gifted instructors.

The work is done with the quiet consistency of the expert. First the slow, progressive and scientific education of the horse, which will make him fit, extremely supple and absolutely obedient; in short, in a condition to enjoy his jumping, to learn to understand it and to become a great performer, capable in some cases of observing and assessing the obstacles.

At the same time the rider's seat, particularly in relation to jumping, and his actions at the approach, the take-off, the period of suspension and the landing, have all been scientifically thought out and the rider is trained until they are almost automatic. The sequence of the rider's movements must have a certain balance or rhythm not easily disturbed by unexpected difficulties. And when he is ready to do so he must learn to ride any number of different courses with the maximum of appreciation of their difficulties and the minimum of movement likely to disturb or unbalance the horse. At this stage the ability to give and take—delicately, decisively or swiftly—is acquired. As a result of this training of both horse and rider you achieve the perfect combination of the two.

Quite often the prospective show-jumping horse has already been backed, broken and used in some capacity before he commences on this new facet of his career. In some cases this can be an advantage. Take Lucky Strike, who won continuously in the hack classes, trained and produced by Count Robert Orssich and ridden to perfection by Annie Davy. He had already been well-schooled before he became a successful show jumper. Few horses ever forget a sound and thorough early education unless of course they get into bad hands and become confused or soured or crafty.

If, however, their way of life has not included much schooling then at all costs they must receive some quiet, consistent, continuous dressage or training. They must fully accept the bit, understand and obey the aids and give carried out simple dressage movements long enough to profit by them physically, to be able to use every bit of themselves to the fullest advantage and to become handier and more supple than would be the case under any other form of preparation, including that used in the exercising and conditioning of the hunter or point-to-point horse.

Properly schooled they will also be more obedient. Imagine to yourself the many ways in which instant obedience is necessary in a difficult competition, including a willingness to jump the exact part of an obstacle at an angle deemed best by the rider. As part of this athletic training a certain amount of circling is valuable for various reasons, including getting the head into the best position and making the horse more ready to use either leading leg, without special preference for one or the other.

When the horse is trained for a show-jumping career from the start and dressage has automatically been part of his curriculum, then he should work over cavallettis and be introduced gradually to jumping various easy obstacles, both on the lunge and when ridden. Riding across country will make him observant and able to use his own initiative when necessary—after all it is part of his natural way of life. It also prevents boredom from too much routine. Some hunting is excellent providing that he has already learned obedience over artificial jumps, which otherwise he might despise. The late Col Joe Hume Dudgeon once said that 'We must teach our horse to be accurate and we must teach him a technique ... What trainers do not always fully realise is that it is up to the trainer to make the horse understand what is required; once he understands and is given the correct indication he seldom fails us.'

Show-jumpers certainly come in all shapes but by and large

147

the horse around 16hh is probably the best proposition. Sometimes you will see quite common horses doing very well but the horse with quality, strong loins and a good head and neck is the most likely to succeed. In fact you cannot fail to observe some really superb horses among the show-jumpers, and their beauty added to their courage and grace of movement make them enthralling to watch when in action in the ring. Most of them are great individuals.

What is so amazing is the astronomical figure the successful show-jumper will fetch now. The highest price paid to date is well over £50,000. Yet between the two wars animals which turned out very well have been bought for as little as five pounds.

A remarkable horse bought by Phyllis Hinton cost between £30 and £40. He was unusual to look at, yet his conformation was good and he was remarkably well schooled, could and would change leading leg alternately at a canter the entire width of a big field without a mistake even when ridden by a novice and was able to carry out both simple and some of the more advanced dressage movements in perfect harmony. He could also show-jump surprisingly well and when lined up for his rosette he seemed to be thrilled to pieces—in fact one felt that he expected to stand even higher than he did. She bought him from a dealer who seemed to know a little about him and never learnt his history.

It is still possible, however, to pick up the untrained horse with a pop in him for a moderate price if one is prepared to take the chance and give the time to preparing him. A costly business, as the care and feeding of horses has also rocketed.

When the competitor walks the course before any big contest he will have first studied the plan and conditions, which are pinned up outside. Frequently he will follow exactly the route he intends to take and may well memorise it very carefully for two reasons: to ensure that he will not make the fatal mistake of taking the wrong course and that he will know it well enough to be able to give all his attention to his horse. It will also help him to estimate distances.

He needs to plan how best to approach any obstacle, the direction in which to continue and the condition of take-off and landing. So much can depend on the way the fences are placed in relation to one another and a clever course builder will make this sufficiently tricky without asking too much of a horse. Incidentally one sure way of losing a horse's confidence is to make a fool of him. Building courses is the work of a talented craftsman who tries to prepare the course to suit the competition and the class of show-jumper competing. Too easy a one is useless and uninteresting; too severe a one is pointless and unfair. A varied course which does not produce too many clear rounds and thus prolong the jump-off is a very practical solution. The man or woman who walks it has to estimate and plan for all the difficulties.

No show-jumping horse can remain at his peak for more than a certain time, therefore the fact that on some occasion he is not jumping with his usual brilliance does not necessarily mean that he is on the downgrade. Given a chance he will be back on form again and it can be irritating to his owner or rider if he gets a bad press.

There is always the thrilling element of chance which means that the round of every single rider is fraught with excitement. But it can be both disconcerting and surprising. The example which comes most immediately to mind is that of Beethoven, ridden by Douglas Bunn, owner of the All-England Jumping Course at Hickstead. The horse jumped magnificently in the competition for the King George V Gold Cup at the Royal International Horse Show, a clear round until he came to the water when, astonishingly, he put a foot in it—and this in spite of the fact that he was a 'natural' at jumping water, being well used to the width of this obstacle at Hickstead, about 16ft and

149

probably the biggest in the country. Beethoven jumped the more difficult fences with apparent ease but threw away his chance of the cup when we least expected it. Herr Gunter Winkler beat him for first place with the eight-year-old horse, Fortun.

The big international competitions such as the King George V Gold Cup are competed for under Table A in the programme. The speed of the Gold Cup is 382 yards per minute and it is stated that in the event of equality of faults for first place there will be a jump-off and in the event of further equality of faults for first place there will be a second jump-off, in which time will decide. Competitors which tie for lower awards not taking part in the jump-off will divide the prize money.

There are many other immensely thrilling and important show-jumping competitions, including the Queen Elizabeth II Cup, which is for lady riders only, just as the King George V is for men only—both these events are held at the Royal International Horse Show. And varied and entertaining ones such as the Rescue Relay, The Accumulator, Gamblers' Stakes, Timed Touch and Out, and so on.

But since we are all out to back our own team to beat the world, one event with a strong national and international flavour is the Nations Cup, known over here as the Prince of Wales Cup, and the equivalent of this international team competition takes place in Ireland (the Aga Khan Trophy), and in many other countries. It is for four riders of the same nationality, certified by the National Federation as eligible to represent the nation. The winning team is that which has the least number of faults when the best three horses of each team are added together at the end of each round—there are two rounds in all.

One remembers with what anxiety and breath-taking anticipation we used to watch each member of our team compete in

Page 151 (*above*) Harvey Smith and O'Malley, both in top form at Hickstead; (*below*) Marion Coakes (Mrs Douglas Mould) on Stroller. Although only 15hh he has won many big international events, including the British Jumping Derby at Hickstead and winning the silver medal in the Individual Show-jumping Grand Prix at the Mexico Olympic Games in 1968

Page 152 (*above*) The great champion hackney pony, Marden Finality, moving magnificently in-hand. He is owned by Miss Rowena Davidson; (*below*) Mr J. E. Seabrook from New Jersey, USA, driving his very fine team of grey Holstein horses at the Richmond Royal Horse Show, where he won the William H. Moore Championship Gold Cup

the days before we had as many experienced riders and good show-jumpers as we have now. Now we are not quite as anxious or as thrilled in spite of the importance of the contest which, incidentally, is over a longish and impressive course—a straightforward one which is in no way confusing to a horse. It has helped to bring to this country and to the other countries in which it takes place many gifted international horses and riders. To observe them has been an education.

One doubts whether any other sport owes as much to a single individual as show-jumping does to Colonel Sir Michael Ansell, CBE, DSO. Like many of our other great show-jumping men he represented Great Britain when riding in our pre-war army teams. The colossal price of show-jumping horses today is in sharp contrast to the actual cash value of the horses which many of them trained and rode between the wars when the top price for an officer's charger was £70 and £40 for a troop horse.

From the time he returned, nearly blind, from a German prisoner-of-war camp until the present day he has worked with unceasing dedication towards the creation of show-jumping as a sport of great national and international importance, run with unanimity and correctness enlivened by healthy competition. The men and women who helped him to achieve this all did an immensely valuable job of work, but without his tremendous enthusiasm, his appreciation of the variety and the unconformity of the human race and of the difficulties with which he would be faced plus his knowledge and experience, one feels that the inspiration would have been missing and less would have been achieved.

All competitions except those with their own specific rules are now judged under Table A or Table S (Speed). Table A is used for all competition except those in which penalties are converted into seconds. In these Table S is used. Winners under Table A are decided by one of the following methods:

153

J

Table A1—in the event of equality of faults for first place in the second jump-off the prize money will be divided.

Table A2—in the event of equality of faults for first place in the second jump-off time will decide.

Table A3—in the event of equality of faults for first place in the first jump-off time will decide. In the event of equality of faults and time in the jump-off, if the judge decides that a further jump-off is essential the course will not exceed six obstacles.

Table A4—in the event of equality of faults for any award in the first round of the competition time will decide. In the event of equality of faults and time for first place, if the judge decides that a further jump-off is essential the course will not exceed six obstacles. Faults are marked as follows:

First disobedience in a round	3 faults
Second disobedience	6 faults
Third disobedience	Elimination
Obstacle knocked down	4 faults
Horse and/or rider falls	8 faults
Exceeding time allowed	$\frac{1}{4}$ fault for each second or part of a second
Exceeding the time allowed in a timed jump-off	1 fault for each second or part of a second
Exceeding the time limit	Elimination

Rules and regulations of the British Show Jumping Association have come into being as a result of experience and are extremely just. It is impossible to enumerate them all but they are published each year and are available to members at the

British Show Jumping Association (see p188).

Quite a few faults are penalised by elimination. Starting before the start signal is given is one, napping or disobedience at an obstacle for more than sixty seconds is another, and taking the wrong course is a third, although if a rider after missing an obstacle returns to the correct obstacle before he jumps or attempts to jump another it will only be faulted as for a disobedience, ie refusal. If an unbroken track is marked on the course plan it must be followed. Another mistake penalised by elimination is jumping an obstacle which does not form part of the course, either before the start or after the finish. One which is designated as a trial obstacle is considered to be part of the course.

There are also a number of disobediences. Stopping at an obstacle without resistance, without knocking it down and without reining back, followed immediately by a standing jump is not penalised. But if the halt is sustained or if the horse reins back even a single pace, voluntarily or not, a refusal is incurred.

If a competitor knocks down one part of a multiple obstacle and then refuses or runs out at the next part without knocking it down the clock is stopped as for a knock-down resulting from a disobedience. The penalties of eight or ten seconds are applied, according to whether the disobedience occurs at the second, third or subsequent parts of a multiple obstacle.

If a competitor knocks down part of a multiple obstacle and then he and/or his horse falls, with or without a disobedience, the clock will not be stopped until the competitor has remounted. The clock will only be stopped if the obstacle has not been rebuilt in time for the competitor to continue his round. Eight or ten seconds will be added to the total time taken.

Other rules and other 'disobediences' apply to these more complex obstacles but the last two paragraphs give some indication of them and all can be found and studied in the British Show Jumping Association Rule Book.

By and large the high jump is not widely used as a competition partly because it may over-face and also completely spoil a courageous, intelligent horse accustomed to a great variety of courses and obstacles. It is generally accepted that a show-jumper needs to be specially trained for this type of contest. It is unwise to use a valuable performer who wins consistently in the standard jumping competitions in this fashion.

One well-known competitor, now dead, frankly admitted that he had made a mistake in entering his horse, a consistent prize-winner, in a high jump competition—he only did so because he was heavily persuaded to it by his colleagues. The poles were raised several times and eventually the horse crashed through them, injuring himself, and he was never the same again. After a few months it became necessary to retire him.

The obstacle for the high jump must be inclined at an angle of 30 degrees from the vertical, away from the direction from which the horse will approach. It must be not less than 16ft in width, and the bottom part of it closed to a height of 4ft 6in with brushwood, wattle hurdles or similar material, to give an impression of stability. Above this are poles, which must be light, covered with a binding of straw and fall easily, 10cm in diameter and set not more than 10cm apart. The wings must always exceed the height of the obstacle by at least a foot.

Faults are as follows:

Obstacle knocked down with hind legs	1 fault
Obstacle knocked down with fore legs	2 faults
Each disobedience	2 faults

Running out, falling or circling do not count.

If the top pole does not fall, even though any lower pole of

156

the obstacle falls, the horse is considered to have cleared it. Each horse is entitled to three trials at each height; a disobedience counts as a trial. Any horse which has cleared the obstacle at one of the three trials is eligible to compete at the following height, and the winner is the horse which clears the greatest height, whatever faults he may have incurred at previous heights.

If more than one horse clears the same height the prizes may be divided *only* if a jump-off has been tried at the next height. If this jump-off gives no result, and no horse has cleared without faults the new height, classification is made on the result of the preceding height cleared without fault, and if necessary in the case of ties, by taking into account the faults made by each horse prior to its clearing the height without fault.

If there are still ties, classification is made by taking into account the faults made at previous heights.

The record achieved by Mr D. Beard riding Mr F. W. Foster's Swank at Olympia in 1937 has never been beaten in England or Ireland. Swank cleared 7ft 6½in on this occasion, but never again did he do as well as he feared the jar on landing.

It is a very wise rule that a condition of entry of all shows affiliated to the British Show Jumping Association is that any horse at that show will be submitted to a veterinary examination if such examination is required by the show executive or judge.

The British Show Jumping Association has endeavoured to eradicate the possibility of cruelty in show-jumping by the appointment of competent and vigilant stewards; by a number of definite and specifically worded rules against ill-treatment; and by limiting the heights of the fences to safeguard the horses and ponies in various competitions, as well as by defining the distances between the elements of a combination

157

fence, to make sure that the fence does not become a trap.

Television has made show-jumping a treat which can be enjoyed by those millions of people who cannot regularly attend the big shows. What brings it alive is the way in which a commentator such as Dorian Williams seems to be a part of every thrilling moment of the round and is able to convey so clearly what is happening to his listeners that they feel they are with him in the stadium.

But television, although a great boon, cannot quite provide the atmosphere, the colour and the emotion of the actual event. To watch the horse and rider of your choice jump a breath-taking round in one of the big competitions while you wonder which obstacle will prove to be the most dangerous hazard; and then to see the winner standing alone, floodlit, in front of all the runners-up to receive the hard-won award to the music of thunderous applause, is a moment of which not all the magic can be conveyed to you by the best television in the world. I think that often the horses are as triumphant as their riders . . . at least they sense the atmosphere of success.

12

Harness Horses

The rallies of the British Driving Society at the various shows provide a wonderful panorama of every imaginable type of horse or pony in harness, many of the latter doing their job quite perfectly. The four-in-hands—private coaches (probably park drags), road coaches of considerable variety, and regimental coaches of the Household Cavalry or Royal Corps of Transport—are even more impressive. A dozen or so of these lined up in an arena, or proceeding round the ring at a smart pace with their rosettes while the band plays nostalgic music, is always very popular. And of course the classes for harness horses and ponies provide an arresting, an amazing display of speed, action and virtuosity.

One can become so absorbed by the colour and movement of these events that one does not always pay enough attention to the finer point of judging although this is naturally of vital import to the exhibitors, some of whom have paid a large sum of money to keep their turnout in prime condition and have come a long way.

Horses which go well together, moving in unison and suitable to the vehicle they are drawing and who are in sufficiently hard condition to stand up to the possible hills and miles of the marathon; a thoroughly roadworthy coach in which no detail has been overlooked and which carries the necessary equipment (spare tack, spare parts, tools and so on) which might be needed during a journey in bygone times—all these and more contribute towards success. But there is far more than this to judging a coaching marathon. It requires considerable knowledge and expertise. Different types of horses are used in the teams, providing of course they match in make, shape and size, and for preference (though this is not essential) in colour. You may see teams of Dutch horses, of hackneys, or Irish hunters and possibly even of the good old-fashioned Cleveland Bay type. To make up a good team today is not easy.

Coaches were designed for a multitude of purposes, some severely practical, others for elegance and comfort—combined, of course, with durability. Information about coaching classes and events can be obtained from the secretary of the Coaching Club.

The turnouts in the rallies of the British Driving Society (see p189) also require expert judging. You may notice how well some of the horses will go, either singly or in pairs, answering immediately to the lightest touch on the rein, moving with considerable dash but always perfectly under control. Here again the horse or pony which covers the largest amount of ground with his stride, rather than displaying too much action but making little progress, is at a considerable advantage. But he most certainly must have action, get his feet well off the ground and literally eat it up, moving equally well both in front and behind.

You will see a variety of carriages and traps in these rallies. Her Majesty the Queen sent a demi-mail phaeton to a pair of horses, driven by Col John Miller, DSO, MC, on one occasion. This is an elegant affair, capable of carrying a fair amount of luggage and with a seat in the rear, the front seats having also a hood which can be raised and lowered. The front wheels are smaller than those at the back, and it is hung on elbow springs behind and elliptic springs in front.

The Victorian pony chaise is perhaps a more cosy vehicle and so is the basket phaeton; both are low to the ground with bodies made of basket work and drawn by sturdy, friendly ponies. They are easy to get into and ideal for children. A two-wheeled dogcart is a vehicle which can bowl along quite quickly. The driver and his companion are in front and two other passengers can be carried if they sit with their backs to them. Originally they had slats on both side as they were intended to transport sporting dogs. There are also four-wheeled dog carts, which can be driven to a single horse or take a pair if required.

The governess cart is really a family tub, useful for a picnic or shopping. It is fairly low to the ground and round in shape, with a small door at the back through which the drivers and passengers enter and sit sideways. If the tub is properly balanced by people and parcels, the driver can sit towards the back and turn towards the way he is going. It is always important to make sure the shafts of any trap are parallel with the ground, not bearing down too heavily on the horse or pony or lifting him off his feet.

The ralli cart is not as high from the ground as the dog cart and is looked upon as an off-shoot of the former, with shafts inside the body instead of under it. There is often a large assortment of gigs present and this is a very comfortable two-wheeled vehicle, well-sprung and sometimes with a hood which can be raised or lowered. The cocking cart is quite arresting and unusual, with a boot in front and a high seat like a box seat of a coach over it, but practically nothing behind. Originally it had slatted panels on each side of the box and is supposed to have been used for carrying fighting cocks.

161

One vehicle which has yet to appear on the show ground is a dormeuse. Luggage could be carried on top of the hood, there was a box and covered rumble seats behind, and inside it was a double-springed sleeping carriage in which one could rest on soft pillows, covered with an eiderdown.

The barouche is a most graceful carriage on four wheels which has a shallow body, and a pair, four or six horses can be used. In the past it was sometimes owner-driven and could be driven from the box or else ridden postillion. Victorias and broughams also make their appearance, the latter a comparatively small, neat, enclosed carriage, the former an open, low-hung, four-wheeled vehicle without doors and very useful in the summer.

The Hackney Horse Society (see p189) holds its own shows, both in-hand and driven events. In addition to these fixtures there are many classes and championships for hackney horses and ponies of various heights, in single harness, pairs and tandems, at all the bigger shows. Straight, strong action and full use of the hocks are of the utmost importance in a harness horse, and he must not break from the trot but apply all his energy to consistent action at this pace. Thus, he is obviously best suited to drawing any vehicle and its passengers, and to the work on the roads for which he was originally intended.

The larger hackney must have a grand, imposing way of carrying himself as well as staying power, substance but no coarseness, plenty of quality and a fine sweep of outline all enhanced by liberty of action. A high action is essential to the hackney rather than the ordinary ride and drive horse or pony, as he is bred, trained and one might say shod with this in mind. As regards a hackney pony, when watching his action remember that it must be dainty and correct and full of force. In both animals look for good loins, ribs, quarters, second thighs, big flat bone and depth through the heart.

The hackney must move with a certain flashing brilliance

which is a joy to witness, and the gift of persuading him to give a high quality performance is an accomplishment only vouchsafed to some drivers. But apart from the professional experts quite a few amateurs own and drive their horses or ponies to victory in the hotly contested classes. The prefixes of various studs have become world-famous and the names of some of the greatest mares and stallions are spoken of with the deepest respect and admiration.

13

Riding Club Teams, Equitation Classes and Some Words of Advice

When one reflects upon the great variety of competitions available at shows one cannot fail to admire the ingenuity and imagination of the organisers. There is something to interest and entertain every class and type of rider, rich or poor, young or old.

Some of the events, such as that for the veteran horse are self-explanatory. This particular class can bring out of retirement a few famous animals as well as others who may not necessarily have been star performers in any particular branch of equitation, but who have led a remarkably interesting life, most of it devoted to the service of their masters or mistresses.

We have not devoted a separate chapter to the classes for riding club teams as much of the material or advice likely to be of use to members already appears in other chapters. The rules for these classes are usually as follows: Riders must be over 17 years of age (the reason for this definite age limit is because those young people who should be, or already are, members of the local branch of the Pony Club might compete in these events which are intended for adults). They must be bona fide members of the riding club which they represent and the horse must be their property, or be owned by the same club, or by a member of that club, or by a riding school normally used by the club.

The class is often judged in three parts:

1 Condition and cleanliness of horse and saddlery. The judges examine the saddlery and award marks for cleanliness and state of repair. The horse must be clean, well trimmed and shod but conformation is not taken into account.

2 The turnout of the rider. Judges take into consideration general cleanliness but not the value of the clothes, although the rider must be suitably turned out. Correct dress: bowler hat, hunting tie, dark coat, breeches and boots.

3 The test. Each team is required to give a short show of their own choice lasting approximately two minutes. After this show they are expected to canter round the ring and jump two small fences as a team. Any team deemed by the judges not to have jumped will be eliminated.

The marks are awarded as follows: horse and saddlery 15, rider 15, display 50, jumping 20.

To achieve good marks requires a lot of work on the part of the riding club members. We will assume that they are already passable riders, their horses in good condition and well trained. All very important points which require sound, consistent outings to prevent boredom and nappiness in the horses. But it is no easy job for members who are at work every day to keep this standard up.

Fortunately many of the clubs are helped by first-class visiting instructors who keep them interested and show them what can be achieved. They hold their own minor shows, hunter trials and so forth with the utmost efficiency, all of which add to their enjoyment and are of particular value to the novice.

One of the greatest problems in preparing for a team event is to find the right time for all three members to get together and practise *keeping* together, as well as carefully timing the display they intend to give. It is also a good thing to get the horses used to music, possibly with the aid of a loud-speaker.

Sometimes the horses in the teams are very cleverly matched in colour, in shape, size and type and in way of going. If this can be achieved it makes the exhibitors' task easier. Horses are sensitive to the atmosphere of a show ring, the impact of the crowds of onlookers and even possibly the nervousness and anxiety of their own riders. Fortunately it is usually possible for them to move about and settle down before the moment comes when they actually enter the arena.

Equitation classes often attract large entries. If this is the case it often happens that they are divided into sections and the judges choose a few of the best from each section and let them compete in a final.

These classes are popular and well organised in Canada. The Canadian Rule Book speaks of three sections: the saddle, hunter and stock seat. In the last section the riders are judged on seat, hands, performance of horse and rider and suitability of horse to rider. Some of the suggested rules for displays in this section correspond to a certain extent to those in the classes for Western Horsemanship given in Chapter 10.

In England the judges in an equitation class for younger children note the position of the rider's body (well down in the saddle), knees (close to the saddle), heels (slightly down) and hands (a little lower than the elbows, which should be close to the body but never stiff) which must maintain a pleasing, light contact with no hanging on to the mouth or rough movements of either arms or hands. Before lining up and giving an easy little individual display they must circle the ring at walk, trot and canter, show that they understand the simple aids, have their ponies under control and be able to stop them without causing them to throw their heads.

In the more advanced classes for either older children or young adults it is assumed that they have already achieved a fair standard. Some of the tests are as follows: riding on a straight line; turning on the haunches and on the forehand; change of pace and change of leg at given points; and the collected and extended paces.

A good test of a pony's obedience and the rider's proficiency is the performance of one or two of the simple exercises which were taught at Saumur, the French riding school, such as riding the outline of a square without cutting the corners. Halfway up the side of the square, turn inwards to form a perfect little circle, regaining the side exactly where the pony left it, and continuing round the square.

A more difficult task is a figure-of-eight. Too often the half circle is made too wide and the horse eventually finishes up at quite a different place from where he started. These exercises should first be practised at a walk, and if it is possible to carry them out on a beach the markings on the sand can be ample proof of the neatness or untidiness of the performance.

If the judges decide to ask competitors to change on to each other's horses or ponies—and this can be very revealing—permission should be obtained from the show secretary and, of course, the riders themselves. In the case of young children it is as well to ask the parents if they agree, and if in any doubt, borrow a quiet pony on which each can carry out some small, simple test.

A final word with regard to showing in any class. Remember always that it is your horsemanship and horsemastership which counts, rather than whether you won a prize or not. The art of showing is really a technique which needs to be learnt; one never ceases to learn and to improve with experience. At first it is hard to see just why one's horse is not as good or even better than the one standing higher in the line-up. But little by little you will begin to realise the small imperfections or perhaps just the lack of super-excellence in your own and other horses or ponies.

14

How to Organise a Show

To run a successful show which is enjoyed by exhibitors, officials and onlookers and even produces a profit is quite an achievement. It requires long-term planning, plus an entirely co-operative and responsible group of organisers.

The British Horse Society (see p188) will always advise on insurance against rain, accidents or any other contingency. It is also a help towards the costs if firms can be found who are willing to sponsor the prize money in some of the events in return for announcing their names in the schedules and programmes.

Here are some suggestions which bring excellent results if carefully followed:

1 A sensible choice of classes likely to suit the competitors who live within a twenty-five mile radius of the show. These classes must be clearly described in the schedule.

2 Good judges, who will be asked to handle the events to which they are adapted.

3 Efficient loud-speaker equipment.

K

4   Good prizes.

5   A time-table which is strictly adhered to—a consultation on the night before the show and possibly a division and slight adjustment of classes.

6   A sufficiency of seats, protection against bad weather, refreshment and cloakroom tents, runners, *experienced*, *reliable* and *fully-informed* ring stewards, programme sellers and men on the gates, including an adequate staff to handle car and horse-box parking. In the case of a big show this can be arranged with a professional firm.

7   Rings suitable to the classes which are to be held in them, an ample exercise ring or space, in addition to the collecting ring, both of which should contain a loud-speaker or a field telephone with someone always in attendance. Stabling, or lines for the horses. Water and, if possible, some forage on sale.

8   A sufficiently staffed secretary's tent where the average person will be made to feel welcome and his or her difficulties, from a lost stirrup leather to finding a last-minue rider for a jumping pony, will be adequately dealt with. Where also the inveterate trouble-maker will meet his match!

9   Inspired advertising.

All these things can be adapted to suit the needs of the larger or smaller show. It is by far the best policy to try and stage a show really well, no matter which category it belongs to, even if it is the first time the show has been held and you are a little nervous of the financial results. Good common sense should save you from any foolish commitments!

You must bear in mind certain facts. The first is that any show other than a gymkhana or an intimate club affair is in many ways a dealer's window display. This may be unpalatable, but it is inescapable, and modern conditions are not likely to bring about a change. Most people are ready to pay a handsome price for a horse that has won in good company, or is likely to win; and quite a large number of competitors who are by no means professional dealers help to cover their expenses by an occasional lucky deal.

In addition to this, many of the more important dealers are literally the backbone of the show ring and their contribution is particularly valuable. Not only do they provide the cream of the entries, ridden and shown by experts, but give practical help in providing prizes and useful contacts.

The novice and the private owner rely upon the show ring to educate or keep them up-to-date, and they are always interested to see the type and quality of the horses competing each year. Many of these people prefer to enter at two or three of the better class shows in fairly good company than at a number of indifferent ones.

From these facts you will no doubt deduce the importance of making sure that your show is properly run, so that it will make a name for itself, both with good horsemen and with the general public.

You will be well advised to take care that while offering the general public every attention and suitable entertainment or displays, you do not include such dubious attractions as flapping races; or roundabouts in close proximity to the ring. Let the horse show maintain its old sporting traditions—it degenerates very quickly when it loses them. Tents filled with fruit, flowers and vegetables are eminently suitable and nearly everyone enjoys the addition of agricultural and horticultural classes.

The financial success of a show is often partially dependent upon the date chosen—if you can manage to book the Saturday preceding one of the best-known early shows, such as for example the Royal Windsor, you can be assured of a good number of entries from competitors anxious to try their horses in the ring before taking part in the bigger show. Furthermore you will be able to profit by the wave of enthusiasm which

K*

usually greets the opening of the show season.

Another very good tip is to try and arrange to hold it on approximately the same date every year, as your 'customers' will acquire the habit of looking forward to it. For instance, you can tie it up with the big show or the race which it precedes, emphasising that the so-and-so show is always held the week before, perhaps, Windsor or Ascot, or what you will.

Now let us elaborate on the nine rules mentioned earlier in the chapter.

1 Classes to be held

As regards the choice of classes you must be guided by your locality to a great extent, but not limited by it. Are there a fair number of hunters available? Or young stock, ranging from ponies upwards? What about cobs, hacks, private and trade turnouts, hackneys, Arabs, Anglo-Arabs and, of course, mountain and moorland ponies?

A novice hack is usually looked upon as one 'that has never won a first prize in a hack class prior to 1 January 19—'. The year in which the show is being held is then given.

You may, however, wish to encourage the hacks which are infrequently shown, and which, although good animals, have never won a prize at all. It is quite possible that they may be asked to compete against a number of show animals which have already won first prizes and championships early in the season in question. The easiest way of getting over this difficulty is to stick to the above wording, and to give an additional prize for the best hack which has never won a prize in a hack class. If you are running an open and not a novice event, this extra prize can still be included and is an added encouragement. So are awards for the best local animal within a given radius.

When there is only one height limit, 15.3hh, an extra prize is sometimes given for the best hack of 15hh or under.

172

While conforming to the correct ruling for all your classes you must do everything you can to make things easy and enjoyable for your competitors. The rules were made to help and protect your competitors, although they may seem irksome and not entirely apposite; but they were evolved for excellent reasons which are not always fully realised. They are a framework upon which you can build, and a few additional prizes are excellent bricks to be added to the edifice of your show!

The height limit for the cob class is defined in Chapter 4; hunter weights are outlined in Chapter 7. If you intend to hold two or three hunter events it is essential to include a clause to the effect that animals competing in one weight class cannot compete in another.

Young stock and brood mare events should be encouraged and there are a variety of classes to choose from. You can have open yearling, two-year-old, three-year-old and four-year-old classes, or you can add a proviso such as 'likely to make a hunter, hack, polo pony, child's pony'. Ask for the breeding to be sent with the entry whenever possible, and it is better to state the year in which the animal was foaled, than simply 'four-year-old' or whatever ages you have decided upon.

If you include Arab, Anglo-Arab or part Arab classes, make sure that the entrants are registered in their respective stud books. The Arab Horse Society (see p188) will help you here. Any kind of Arab display is a great draw.

Ponies and jumping classes will probably bring the biggest number of entries. The rule which prevents our hunter entering in two weight classes should prevail with regard to the ponies' heights—it may prevent some bitter disappointments. All you need say in your schedule is 'for ponies exceeding such-and-such a height and not exceeding so-and-so', instead of simply stating 'for ponies not exceeding so-and-so'. Write to the British Show Pony Society for advice and for its booklet.

173

Remember that the pony class which is judged 50 per cent on the riding ability of the child is usually fair to neither, nor is a prize for the best child rider to be recommended. It is far better to hold two distinct classes, one for the pony, and one for equitation, when both can be properly and carefully judged. An age limit must certainly be imposed in equitation classes.

When planning your pony events it is as well to take note of whether your show date is likely to clash with any school events. If it is held during the holidays this question will not arise, but it is a serious consideration during term-time. It is also advisable to make some arrangement, such as a special cup, or class, or seats, for Pony Club members. Have a talk with your local District Commissioner, who may prove helpful and co-operative.

You may decide to include a class for mountain and moorland ponies; or offer a prize for the best native pony competing in any of the events. In either instance you must insist on your schedule that the pony's registered number is sent with the entry, or you will find that many doubtful ponies will take part, to the annoyance of the genuine exhibitor. Sometimes these native pony classes include every known breed; sometimes they are confined to one breed alone, such as the Welsh or Dartmoor. The ponies can be shown in-hand, or ridden; but the classes should be open to adult as well as juvenile riders.

Both hackney and private turn-out classes greatly enhance the appearance of the ring and have a definite entertainment value. The hackneys flash by with brilliant display of speed and spirit, and the delightful horses and ponies drawing high-wheeled gigs, dog-carts, chaises and the useful but humble governess cart, all add immensely to the day's enjoyment. In this connection you should contact the Hackney Horse Society in the one instance and the British Driving Society in the other (see p189).

The riding school class is another event with great possibilities. Not only is it very interesting to watch, but it inspires children and grown-ups to superhuman efforts and provides them with an object for their endeavours. Riding-school work is often difficult and disheartening and many good schools have done immense service in keeping the flag flying during the difficult war years. Most of their excellently trained horses cannot be spared for showing in the ordinary way, or may not have the perfect conformation necessary, but in this event they get a chance to acquire some of the honours due to them.

The schools can also give pupils evidence of their value, and make it easier for the novice rider to compare their pupils' performance and that of their horses before deciding where to go for instruction. This is particularly important in view of the many bad schools which have come into being, and which do so much harm to the good name of the horseman. The best wording for this event is 'for teams of three, riding master or mistress with two bona fide pupils. Horses must have been the property of the school for at least three months prior to the date of entry; 25 per cent each for conformation, manners, riding ability and turn-out of rider.'

A class for teams of members of riding clubs is worthy of consideration; also for family teams of one adult and two young people.

You may decide to include a combined training event, or a dressage or a Prix Caprilli Test. The excellent booklet referred to in Chapter 6 and entitled *Dressage Rules and Official Procedure for Dressage Competitions,* published by the British Horse Society, will help you here. So will the various tests as well as the leaflets on the Prix Caprilli Test which are available from the British Horse Society.

Preliminary judging can take place in a separate ring in the morning, which must be far enough away from the main ring to ensure quiet, and the final placing of the first half dozen

175

can be judged in the main ring in the afternoon for the benefit of those people who were unable to be present during the morning. Or the judging can be completed in the correct ring during the morning and the winner be asked to give a short display in the afternoon.

If two judges officiate at a dressage test it is as well to place them at separate tables a little distance apart, and each should have a writer available. Some will bring their own writers with them. Judge's table, chairs, papers, assistant and runners should all be placed in a good position in the ring. A megaphone and loud-speaker should be available and a full description of the class posted on a board at the entrance. A good announcer should explain the test to the onlookers before the event starts, besides giving the name of each horse as it enters the ring. If there are many competitors a slight break should be made halfway through the event to allow the announcer to repeat his explanation to late-comers.

There should always be plenty of rosettes available in case the judges find some special reason for asking for extra ones. It is also a good idea to have a board standing in each ring clearly stating the class number and of what consists, ie hacks not exceeding 15.3hh or cobs, or whatever it may be. This should be changed without the slightest delay directly a new class enters the ring. These boards are a great help to all who attend the show.

Now comes the question of the jumping events. Usually they delay the programme considerably; or alternatively the unfortunate jumpers have to wait about for a considerable length of time. The best solution to this problem is to arrange a separate ring for jumping only, if this can in any way be managed. It will enable you to take many more entries and to run your jumping classes far more comfortably for all concerned.

If it is not feasible to devote one ring to jumping only, then you must choose the best classes, and decide beforehand exactly how many jumpers may compete in each class. You can state on your schedule the closing date for jumping entries and the fact that you are only able to accept a specified number. Stage the best jumping class, such as the open adults or touch-and-out, or the open juvenile, at a time when most onlookers are likely to be present. Hold the novice or Foxhunter classes, which are apt to become monotonous, at a less popular hour.

A good jumping course need not be big, if the jumps are properly spaced and set at the best angle to one another. A most impressive course, which is actually not difficult to jump, is easily constructed with a little imagination.

The great thing to guard against is having space between the bottom rail of the jump and the ground. Fill it with flowers, or with anything you like, but be sure to fill it. Have plenty of spread jumps, and place something in the way of a take-off in front of your more difficult high jumps. The horses will jump 100 per cent better, the ring look far nicer, and the competitors and onlookers enjoy themselves twice as much.

The British Show Jumping Association (see p188) is most useful in this respect, and as it is not so important that jump judges should be called in from a different district, the association can often recommend the services of people living within easy reach of the show ground.

All shows should be affiliated to this association, which will be of inestimable help as regards planning jumping courses, procuring jumps, awarding prizes and in a myriad other ways. The assistance of the area representative is always available.

2 Judges

Good or bad judges will make or mar a show. Now that shows are bigger, entries more numerous and classes clearly defined and specialised than ever before it is unfair to ask too much of your judges—three or four classes are usually enough, particularly if this number includes jumping classes.

There are three golden rules:

1 Have your judges' names on the schedule as well as the programme, if possible stating which classes they will be handling.

2 Do not have more than two judges in each class, but arrange for some suitable person to be called as referee if required. Make sure that your two judges are prepared to work together—it is essential to find out if the judges chosen are on good, or at least not bad, terms with one another!

3 Invite judges from outside the area in which the show is held. The good judge will probably know quite a lot of the horses in his own district, and he is often wrongly accused of bias. Furthermore, the name of a judge from some distance away usually adds interest to the schedule. It has a bracing effect and often helps to prevent the organisers and committee from getting into a rut.

The question of payment often arises. There is no fixed rule on this point, although it is usual to refund a judge's out-of-pocket travelling or hotel expenses. Some make a present of their services to the charity for which the show is run. It is usual to enquire their wishes on this point.

It is most important to allocate to them the events which they are best adapted to judge. Some excellent hunter judges are quite unsuited to hack classes. The hackney judge is clearly a specialist, and so is the children's pony judge. If in any doubt as to the best people to contact, the organiser should write to the society which caters for the type of horse in question, and ask for advice.

3 *Loudspeaker*
Book your loudspeaker equipment well in advance, get the best people available, explain the lie of the land to them and

178

let them decide how to make the most of it—they know their own job better than you do.

You will require field telephones from the judge in the field to the announcer at the microphone, if this is feasible. You will then be able to announce the results while the rosettes are being handed round and give the names of the horse, his owner and his rider, in addition to the number. During the jumping classes the faults can be announced immediately the round is completed.

Should a field telephone be out of the question you must supply a stream of efficient runners, or a new variety of tic-tac man! A large wooden results board standing perhaps 15 or 20ft in height, with coloured rosettes beside the winning numbers to indicate first, second and third, is an excellent idea. It is most essential to enter the results on any results board with the least possible delay.

Explain to the engineer in charge of your equipment that you want the loudspeaker adjusted to interfere with the horses as little as possible, and leave him to take the appropriate steps. There should be a microphone in use in each ring, and in the collecting ring too, as this will speed things up and make it easier to contact the competitors.

When records are played make sure that they are suitable to the class in the ring at that time, and that they are on no account too loud. This can easily be avoided without impairing the enjoyment of anyone on the field if there is sufficient equipment available. Should this not be the case, it is far better to dispense with the music, or make certain that it is not loud, even if this means that it will not be heard in some parts of the ground.

The announcer, if he is not a 'horsey' man, should content himself with giving the necessary information clearly and adequately, without risking too many interpolations of his own, as sometimes the announcer's wise-cracks fall wide of the mark. An occasional dry, humorous remark is a pleasant surprise, but anything else is apt to be wearisome. He can supply descriptions of the animals competing and explanations of the classes if the information is, as it should be, given him from the secretary's tent. But he must on no account speak of the past winnings of a horse until after it has been judged, except in the jumping class.

This brings to mind a very important person, whose services are not always available—the public relations officer. It is certain that the secretary and his assistant, the ring stewards and the judges will all be too busy to fill this important post. But it is equally certain that someone should do it, and the right person can contribute enormously to the success and popularity of the show.

The public relations officer must know every detail connected with each class that is being held, and must be able to answer any question connected with it. He must compile the interesting information with which the microphone man is going to enrich the public. He must be prepared to effect introductions, to smooth over the 'spot of bother' which is almost bound to arise at some time; to see that the judges and officials are suitably 'watered' and fed, and he must make careful notes of improvements which can be inaugurated at the next show.

If you have been fortunate enough to obtain the services of a popular announcer—there are not very many about—you can leave everything to him (or her). Otherwise you will do well to carry out the foregoing instructions.

4 Prizes

There are naturally many conflicting opinions on prizes, their object, use and value. Some people say that big prizes commercialise what should be a sporting event; others that as the competitors provide the interest which attracts the gate it should be made worth their while to enter. Naturally these points can be considerably elaborated and many others added. But in view of the expense of breeding or buying your show horse or pony, feeding, preparing and schooling him, transporting him to the shows and paying his entry fees, the bait of a good cash prize is very tempting.

There are two rules which may help you to steer a wise course. First, if your show is more or less confined to club or inter-club competition it will be best to offer attractive prizes of a utility or souvenir variety. A head-collar which can be put into immediate service, or a book, book-token, sporting print or tie-pin, which will arouse pleasant recollections in years to come, are the most suitable awards. In this case the value of the prize should lie in its quality, good taste, or appropriateness rather than in its cost.

Second, at the bigger, less personal shows, good prize money is essential and the safest main principle is to offer cash prizes in all the events, instead of cups. By all means include a few good challenge cups if you can obtain them, as the possibility of winning a cash prize and a challenge or championship cup greatly enhances the value of the event.

Your cup can either be won outright or if it is a particularly good one let it be a challenge cup which can be competed for yearly, with each winner's name inscribed upon it. Should the same person win it three years in succession it can become his property; or you can state in the programme that it is a perpetual challenge cup, which can never be won outright. A small replica or an engraved medal is usually given to the holder to retain when the cup is returned at the end of his year of tenure.

Except in the case of champion cups, which should be suitably presented, it is far better to advise the winners to collect their awards after each event, rather than await a formal prize-giving.

181

L

Concerning supplementary cups, medals and rosettes, the ring stewards must be asked to make doubly certain that they go to the right people, as so often there is an unfortunate muddle. If, for example, a cup is offered for the best hack that has never won a first prize, the best animal under 15hh or the best native pony in an ordinary children's pony class, the ring steward should make a note of the competitors eligible for these prizes while the class is in the collecting ring or while it is being judged. In some cases, the information should be re-checked at the secretary's tent.

Although good prize money is an undoubted draw, it is not a sole and certain means of bringing in the entries. A popular show with lesser prize money, but with a reputation of sound organisation, friendly atmosphere and reliable judges will usually gain the larger number of entries. This is still more potent if the show has made anything of a name for itself as it is a high recommendation for a horse to be placed at a good show than to have won at an indifferent one.

5 Timing

As far as possible refrain from altering the rotation, or the time, if that has been stated, of the events listed on your schedule. Work out your timetable carefully, allowing enough time for a fair number of the competitors in the more important events to give an individual show and to have their entrants carefully examined. Bear in mind the fact that events in which supplementary prizes are awarded require a greater length of time.

Should you find that any one class is overloaded with entries decide how it shall be divided on the night before the show, the prizes which are to be allocated to it, and the instructions which are to be given to the ring stewards in the morning.

The competitors for the next class should always be collected in plenty of time and should file into the ring at one end, while the class which has just finished goes out at the other. Never allow your ring to stand empty—this is very bad showmanship.

Having done your part to ensure smooth running you must have a word with your judges, explain the time allotted to each class and your plans in connection with it. Discuss any questionable point with them. Beg them to keep up to time, as time lost in one class will have to be made up in another, which is hardly fair. An occasional reminder while the event is being judged is often helpful.

6 *Seating accommodation*

It is absolutely essential to have adequate seating accommodation and shelter from the weather, two things which are far easier to arrange than many people realise. Naturally it is very helpful if you have staged your show on some recreation ground where there are some wooden pavilions. If that has not been feasible and you have to provide your own, there are various alternatives from which to choose.

For instance, many firms will erect temporary covered stands for one day only, and this is often done with great success; or you can hire wooden benches or deck chairs with which you can create enclosures at varying prices; and larger tents or marquees can be put up as a protection against storms. If you do not know the name of a suitable contractor you can probably obtain the information from your Town Hall, or from your firm of caterers.

A humbler alternative, but one which is not to be despised, is to use hay wagons, or graded bales of straw to form a tier of seats. These are surprisingly comfortable and a great protection against wind.

Milk bars, ice-cream merchants, tea tents and licensed bars, in addition to luncheon and buffet tents, should be booked long in advance. At some shows the most excellent refreshments have been provided on a really big scale by members of the committee who have arranged it among themselves. It has involved a tremendous lot of work, but the results have been spectacular.

The cloakroom tents are seldom adequate, and it is rare that an attendant with jug, basin, towels, toilet paper, scissors, pins and aspirin is ever provided, although these are valuable additions to any show. Plenty of programme sellers and ticket men on the gates are another essential.

Even more important is the good collecting ring steward and his assistants. Like the judges, he can make or mar your show. Efficiency, good humour, a real desire to help and a genuine knowledge of horses must be part of his make-up, plus lots of organising ability. He must be ingenious, quick to think, quick to act, and able to size up a situation immediately.

7 *The rings*

Have two, or even three, running if you can, with a space between them which will allow the crowd to surge backwards and forwards, or to turn quickly from one to the other, if it wants to. They must be flat, smooth, and suitable in size to the classes which are to be shown in them—for example, the hunters want plenty of room in which to gallop.

There should be an ample exercise ring or space near, if possible, the collecting ring, and one or two practice jumps are usually very welcome. Arrange to have a loudspeaker or field telephone contacting this ground and the collecting ring. There should be someone always in attendance at the field telephones.

Stabling, shelter of some kind, rope lines for the horses which have not come by box should be available, and, of course, water. Arrange to have some forage on sale if this can be done.

It is also a good thing to encourage stands of various descriptions, such as photographers' displays, saddlery, or anything out of the ordinary, as this will add to the interest, as well as to the receipts of the show. In many cases the stand-exhibitors will pay a fee for the hire of their bit of ground, or make some other useful contribution.

You will also be well advised to make sure that there is a vet in attendance as well as a carpenter and a blacksmith; and it is often a good thing to invite an official from the RSPCA. It is unlikely that his services will be required but the courtesy is one which will be well repaid. It is essential that there should be St John Ambulance or Red Cross attendants available.

Last but not least, a third party policy should be taken out with a good insurance company—some companies will contribute excellent posters advertising the show.

8 *The secretary's tent*

The public relations officer (see p180) will deal with a number of the difficulties which would otherwise harass the secretary, who must at all costs have an assistant and perhaps a runner. The good secretary must have everything at his fingertips, or some impatient person will eventually catch him out. He must be meticulous in the allocation of numbers to competitors: it is best to post these off several days in advance and if the same person has entered several different horses, the name of the horse and class in question should be marked on the back of the card. It is often advisable to post the competitor's and the groom's free admission card together with the numbers, and no one lacking these cards should be admitted without payment. The secretary should obviously be kept informed of everything that happens throughout the day.

If your gate and programme money is likely to reach substantial dimensions it is as well to have it collected at intervals by a responsible person. Your local bank manager should be consulted as he will either arrange to send a representative—

even if it is on a Saturday—or make it possible for you to lodge the money at the bank for the night.

9 *Inspired Advertising*

In addition to buying space in a paper there are many ways of advertising a show which are not always fully explored. But the first essential is to make sure that in your press publicity you tell the public what it wants to know. The following points are the most important:

The type of classes.
Judges and prizes.
The venue, and the best means of getting to it by train, bus or car. A very few words will often save the unfortunate enthusiast a great deal of time and trouble and will ensure his presence when he might otherwise have decided that he had not the time to make the necessary enquiries.

Some indication of these three things should be given in every advertisement and explained more fully on schedules and posters.

Notify the press, and the appropriate association, as soon as your date is decided upon, in the hope that this will avert clashing with other shows. Send details of your activities and a copy of your schedule to each of the 'horsey' periodicals in order that any interesting point may be given due publicity. Invite the attendance of press representatives and photographers and make sure that suitable accommodation is provided for them. In the case of a big show this will include a tent, table and chairs.

Get in touch with the local authority, with your local paper, with everyone you know who is interested in horses, with the boys' and girls' schools; and arrange for posters to be displayed in as many clubs as possible, also a number of shops.

186

On the entry form at the back of your schedule you should have a heading clearly indicating the places where the name of the owner, the horse and rider can be filled in. If the breeding and/or registered number can be included, this is all to the good, and will help you to compile an interesting programme. Directly the schedules arrive from the printers, copies must be sent to the judges, who should also be contacted a few days before and given information about transport and accommodation.

The object of the programme is to provide information as quickly as possible. Therefore make sure that the numbers are in rotation—17, 21, 143, 180, instead of 17, 180, 21, 143—as by this means it will be much easier to find out all about the horse which can only be traced by its number. In the case of an overfilled programme of jumping entries it is quite likely that the animal will have completed his circuit and gone out of the ring before you have discovered who he is, unless the numbers run concurrently.

Include the name of the owner, horse and rider on the programme, adding age, colour and breeding wherever possible. Leave a clearly marked space at the end of each class, into which results can be copied. Half a page or a page devoted to a description of the jumping classes and an explanation of how these classes are faulted, together with a fair-sized space for notes, will help to make the programme worth-while.

Showing certainly has a tremendous future. The man in the street is beginning to appreciate and enjoy some of the finer points, and as it becomes more and more widely understood, so equally will its popularity increase. It is essential that the novice should be given every encouragement to try his hand at showing, and that while plenty of attention is accorded to what one may term the 'shop-window' or commercial side of it, the sporting angle must also be carefully safeguarded.

187

Some Useful Addresses

Arab Horse Society
Secretary: Lt-Col J. A. Denney ERD, Sackville Lodge,
Lye Green, nr Crowborough, Sussex

British Driving Society
Secretary: Mrs P. Chandler, 10 Marley Ave, New Milton,
Hampshire

British Horse Society
Secretary: J. E. Blackmore, the National Equestrian Centre,
Stoneleigh, Kenilworth, Warwickshire CV8 2LR

British Palomino Society
Secretary: Mrs P. Howell, Kingsettle Stud, Cholderton,
Salisbury, Wiltshire

British Show Hack and Cob Association
The National Equestrian Centre

British Show Jumping Association
The National Equestrian Centre

British Show Pony Society
Secretary: Capt R. Grellis, Smale Farm, Wisborough Green,
nr Billingshurst, Sussex

British Spotted Horse and Pony Society
Secretary: Miss J. Eddie, Nashend, Bisley, Stroud,
Gloucestershire

Coaching Club
Secretary: R. A. Brown, 65 Medfield Street, Roehampton,
London SW15

Hackney Horse Society
Secretary: R. A. Brown, 65 Medfield Street, Roehampton,
London SW15

Hunters' Improvement and Light Horse Breeding Society
Secretary: G. W. Evans, 8 Market Square,
Westerham, Kent

Joint Measurement Scheme
Organiser: J. E. Blackmore, the National Equestrian Centre

National Pony Society
Secretary: Cdr B. H. Brown RN, 85 Cliddesden Road,
Basingstoke, Hampshire

Welsh Pony and Cob Society
32 North Parade, Aberystwyth, Cardiganshire

Western Horseman's Association of Great Britain
Hon Secretary: Mrs R. Hicks, Round Close, Yately,
Camberley, Surrey

Index

Page numbers in italics indicate plates

191